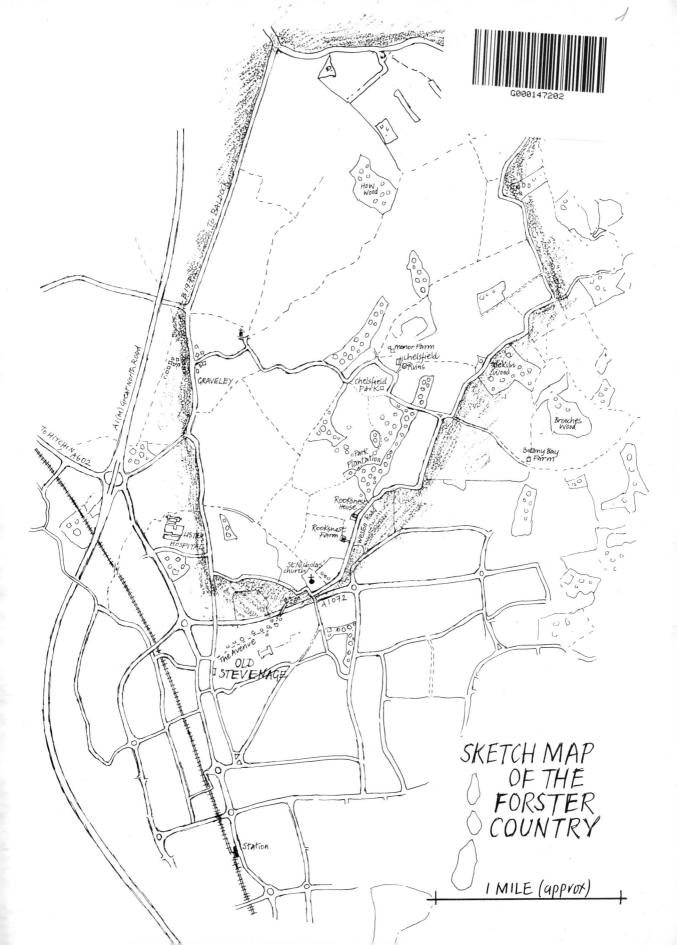

SKETCH MAP
OF THE
FORSTER
COUNTRY

1 MILE (approx)

FORSTER
COUNTRY

FORSTER COUNTRY

Margaret Ashby

Flaunden Press

Dedication
for
all friends of the Forster Country
and
to the memory of
Elizabeth Poston
genius loci

Flaunden Press
Old Town Books, 94 High Street, Stevenage, Herts SG1 3DW
Printed in Great Britain by A.H. Dunn (Printers) Ltd

CONTENTS

Illustrations credits

Cover: Water-colour painting by Alan Burgess

Endpapers: Map of the Forster Country by Audrey Hammond
Inventory of the estate of John Howard, died 1767

Numbers 8, 9, 11, 12, 14, 19, 21, 27, 29, 31, 34, 41, 46, 47, 49, 52, 54 by Audrey Hammond.

Numbers 3, 4, 5, 10, 18, 20, 30, 32, 35, 36, 43, 44 reproduced by permission of the Provost and Scholars of King's College, Cambridge.

Numbers 6, 7, 15, 17, 24, 25, 28, 37 courtesy of Stevenage Museum.

Numbers 1, 26, 50, 51, 52 by Bill Smith.

Number 2 courtesy of Hertfordshire County Record Office. Number 13 courtesy of John Austin. Number 33 by Jack Franklin. Numbers 16, 38, 39, 40, 42, 48 courtesy of James Poston. Number 45 courtesy Babs Franklin. Numbers 55 and 56 by Betty Game.

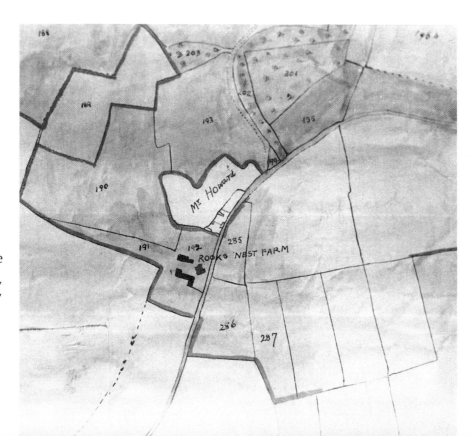

2. Chesfield estate Map c. 1819, showing "Mr Howard's."

INTRODUCTION

Small is beautiful. Never have these words been more apt than when applied to the Forster Country of North Hertfordshire, which adjoins Rooks Nest, childhood home of the writer E.M. Forster. In *Howard's End*, the novel which draws its inspiration from Rooks Nest, Forster reflects that "ten square miles are not ten times as wonderful as one square mile, that a thousand square miles are not practically the same as heaven." Forster lived at Rooks Nest with his mother from 1883 to 1893, from the age of four to fourteen; a short period for one who lived to be ninety-one, yet those ten years had a profound effect upon the rest of his life. In 1946 he gave a radio talk in which he said, "I was brought up as a boy in a district which I still think the loveliest in England... I have kept in touch with it, going back to it as to an abiding city and still visiting the house which was once my home, for it is occupied by friends..."

The friends to whom he refers were the composer Elizabeth Poston and her mother. Noted for her collections of carols and folk-songs, and for beautiful original compositions such as *Jesus Christ the Apple Tree*, Elizabeth Poston also had a distinguished career with the BBC. Dr Malcolm Williamson, Master of the Queen's Music, said of her, "She regarded herself as a miniaturist and she preferred the smaller forms but nobody is going to criticise a diamond on account of its size..."

The Forster Country may be small geographically, but its influence has been great. It is the aim of this book to recount the story of the Forster Country and of the people whose lives were so closely bound up with it. I have taken a chronological approach, but this is not a comprehensive history, nor a definitive biography. P.N. Furbank has already written a detailed and scholarly life of E.M. Forster. I am concerned here specifically with Forster's childhood and his subsequent association with his old home. The range and greatness of Elizabeth Poston's work is still being uncovered and in due course a music scholar will come forward to write

INTRODUCTION the biography she merits. Like a diamond, she had many facets and it was not given to any one person to see them all. She had innumerable friends and colleagues and I have been able to use contributions from only a few. Very many others have been omitted, not because I am unaware of their value, but through lack of time to contact all those in her world-wide circle. In the hope that they will understand, I offer them this very personal and incomplete portrait of Elizabeth Poston, and one that is rooted in the locality of her own Forster Country.

ACKNOWLEDGEMENTS

I am immensely grateful to the following people for their help in the preparation of this book. Without their generous support and encouragement it could never have been completed.

The Provost and scholars of King's College, Cambridge for permission to quote from letters in the Forster Archive; Michael Halls, former Modern Literary Archivist at King's, for help over many years; Simon Campion of Campion Press for permission to quote from the works of Elizabeth Poston, and for much help; the staff of the Hertfordshire County Record Office; the staff of Hitchin and Stevenage Museums; my colleagues at Hertford Regional College Library; the staff of Stevenage Central Library; Alan Burgess; Mary Fisher; Babs Franklin and Doris Guest, daughters of Frank Franklin; Betty Game; Ruby Game; Anne and Albert Haggar; the late Mrs Winifred Haggar; Audrey Hammond; John and Angela Hepworth; Steven Hodges; Jackie Madden, Assistant Librarian at the British Film Institute; Anne Mariner; John Morgan; John Morris of Old Town Books, Stevenage; Ken Poole; James Poston; Robin Poston; Keith Robinson; Suzanne Rose; Bill Smith; Gunnvor Stallybrass; Peter Taylor; Norman Thomas di Giovanni; Malcolm Williamson; and many other good friends in "the Rooks Nest family."

PROLOGUE
THE HOWARDS

"In these English farms, if anywhere, one might see life steadily and see it whole, group in one vision its transitoriness and its eternal youth..." (E.M.Forster, *Howards End*, chapter 33.)

From the high point of Rooks Nest, John Howard looked out across his land. In the distance, far beyond his own fields, the blue line of the Chiltern Hills merged imperceptibly with the sky. Behind him was his own house, Howards; red brick, unpretentious, homely. The year was 1764, but it could equally well have been 1664 or 1864. His father and his father's father had farmed here before him, his son and his son's son would follow after. For at least three hundred years there was a John Howard at Rooks Nest, eldest son after eldest son husbanding the land and handing it on to the next generation. Over the centuries oxen had given way to plough horses, open fields were enclosed, seed-drills replaced broadcast sowing, but these changes, important enough in their time, were superficial in the context of such continuity.

Once the Howards had owned Rooks Nest Farm, whose land adjoined their own seventeen acres, but by the early 1700's it had been acquired by the neighbouring Chesfield estate, owned in the eighteenth century by the Sparhauke, or Sparrowhawke, family. An entry in the *Memorandum Book* of Nicholas Cholwell, Rector of Stevenage in 1764, reads: "Rooks Nest - a farm belonging to Laundey and Edward Sparhauke Esq. and rented by John Howard."

Chesfield itself had once been a small village, a parish in its own right, but during the Black Death in the fourteenth century its population was reduced so drastically that it never recovered. All that remained after this terrible plague was the manor house, a few cottages and a little flint church dedicated to St Etheldreda. Not many years later, following a series of disputes about parish boundaries with the neighbouring village of Graveley, the two incumbents so far forgot their Christian calling as to indulge in a bitter fight, which resulted in the death of the Chesfield priest at a place immortalised as Parson's Green. St. Etheldreda's Church stood for three more centuries, surviving the depredations of Cromwell's puritanical zealots during the English Civil War, but by 1750 it was so little used that the Bishop of Lincoln granted a licence allowing it to be demolished. Its "two bellys in the steple" were silenced, no longer to ring out across the empty fields, summoning its tiny congregation. Abandoned to ivy and barn owls, the building gradually fell into ruins, but was never quite deserted by local people, for whom its isolation, coupled with the story of its past history, made it a place of informal pilgrimage.

Although closely associated with Chesfield, Rooks Nest has always been in Stevenage parish, at whose church of St. Nicholas, half a mile down the lane, successive generations of Howards were baptized, married and buried. Their remaining tombstones are close by the south wall, their names recorded in three centuries of parish registers.

The Howards prospered during the eighteenth century, enlarging their holdings by renting glebe and other land. They used some of their profits to rebuild the front of "Howards" and to install fashionable panelled doors in all the rooms. John Howard took a responsible part in Stevenage society, regularly attending the Vestry meetings whose duty it was to administer local government. When he died in 1767, his estate was valued at £2,234..15..8, which compared very favourably with those of wealthy innkeepers and tradesmen in the district.

During the nineteenth century the Howard fortunes seemed to have waned. When the 1861 census was taken, John Howard was recorded as a farmer of seventeen acres, employing one boy. Rooks Nest Farm was now occupied by Gilbert Marsh, a Yorkshireman, who farmed three hundred and eighty acres, employing ten men and five boys. Clearly the Howards were at a low ebb; their farm was probably too small to be economically viable, and with a staff of only one boy, even if supplemented by casual labour, John Howard

10

must have found life hard. Added to this, English farming was entering upon one of its periods of decline, when many of the smaller, less affluent, units would be unable to continue independently. Ten years later, in 1871, there was little change at Rooks Nest. Gilbert Marsh's empire had expanded to four hundred acres, his staff increased to thirteen men and three boys. John Howard, aged sixty-two, and his wife Mary, who was forty-six, were still clinging to their seventeen acres with the help of one boy, while their children, John, aged eleven, Mary Ann, ten, and William, eight, were all attending school.

Ownership of the Chesfield estate had descended to Lieutenant-Colonel Robert Hindley-Wilkinson, through his wife's family. The Wilkinsons were also heirs to tragic misfortune. Their eldest son, Charles, had died at the age of twelve and their second son, Edward, was to be killed in battle in 1879, leaving their daughter Caroline as the only surviving child. In 1881 she became engaged to be married to Charles Poyntz-Stewart of Montague House, Upper Norwood, Surrey and the business of drawing up a marriage settlement began. It was signed on 31st January 1882 and included details of "Rooksnest late Howards Farm" consisting of "house and homestead, home close and malthouse close" together with a total pasturage of four acres, three rods and four perches.

The Howards had gone. Why they left may be guessed at: agricultural decline, the small size of their farm, the age-gap between father and son, all must have been factors. Where they went remains a mystery.

3. E. M Forster aged four, by
J.W Harrison, pupil of Sir
George Richmond

1
SEARCH FOR A HOME

The Important One lay asleep, his golden curls spread over his pillow, at peace in the security of his mother's presence. Christened Edward Morgan Forster after his birth on January 1st 1879, the child was always called by his second name of Morgan and often referred to by his doting family as "The Important One," a nick-name now all the more poignant because his father was dead, having succumbed, like so many of his family, to tuberculosis.

The widowed Lily Forster, Morgan's mother, was only twenty-five when her husband died, leaving her with an infant son. For the next two years she led an unhappy life, sometimes staying at the Clapham house of Marianne Thornton, her husband's wealthy aunt who had befriended Lily when she was a young girl. The kindness and generosity of Aunt Monie, as she was known in the family, was becoming claustrophobic and Lily decided in 1882 that she must get away to lead a life of her own. Coupled with this was her fear that Morgan, who was "delicate", might develop the same illness as his father, and she felt an urgent desire to move out of London into the purer air of the country.

As her son slept, Mrs Forster was writing in some excitement to her great friend and cousin by marriage, Maimie Synnot. She had spent several months house-hunting in the home counties, eventually following up an advertisement which first appeared in the *Hertfordshire Express* newspaper for June 17th 1882;

> "TO BE LET - on lease or otherwise - a SMALL HOUSE, at Rooksnest, Stevenage (unfurnished) containing drawing room, dining room, hall, kitchen, scullery, pantry and larder on ground floor, 4 bedrooms on first floor, good attics, wc etc; excellent cellars. Beautifully situated with extensive views over some of the prettiest parts of Herts. 1/4 mile from Stevenage church and 1 1/4 miles from Stevenage station. Rent £45 or with 4 acres of excellent Pasture £55. Stabling if required. For further particulars inquire of Mr Warren, Jun.,Builder, Stevenage. "

The house seemed ideal for Mrs Forster, particularly when compared with another she had inspected on the same day. She described it all to Maimie:

"19, Peterborough Rd. Bayswater.Tuesday
Dearest Maimie,
Thank you for your very long letter! I do believe I have at last found a house - at least I know I have found it & now it only rests with Colonel Wilkinson the landlord to accept me as a tenant & that he has practically done but I am to know definitely tomorrow. Well now I must begin at the beginning & tell you all about it. Last Tuesday I went to Biggleswade and Stevenage - the former place is in Bedfordshire & more hideous than thought can tell - too frightful. I did not like hurting the feelings of the lady owners of the house but I was obliged to say it was more frightful than I could bear. They sighed and said it was not pretty but very healthy - oh horror - fancy living endlessly gazing at cabbage fields & as a last straw...they said the land around was very good for growing onions - it was an onion country & there was a very pretty cemetary [sic] - so I suppose they meant me to grow onions & then die - I left in despair & went to Stevenage. I was told by the station people the "Rooksnest" was $2^1/_2$ miles from the station & not $1^1/_4$ as the agents said but for once in their lives the agents spoke the truth. I walked through a long avenue & arrived at Stevenage church & my house was about $^1/_4$ mile further on - on the high road about 100 yards from a farm one way and 100 yards from Colonel Wilkinson's lodge the other, it is a very old gabled house and yet it is perfectly new, it has been refurbished, the inside scooped out - everything nice & pretty as possible - good sanitary arrangements. One drawback is I only have rainwater & must get my drinking water from the farm if however I run short of water Co. Wilkinson will sink me a well. The rainwater is filtered before it goes into the tank so it will be very nice for everything except drinking. The rent is £55 with 4 acres of land. I mean to take the land , as it is only grass fields & I shall sell my hay as it stands if I can. I shall have to make a garden... There are two sitting rooms in the house & a large hall & six bedrooms. I should not have chosen to live in such a lonely place if I could have helped it but I can't find anything else & here is winter upon me again. I propose to take the house from Xmas & go in at [?] February so I shall go to Bournemouth for the winter - this I do to appease Monie as otherwise I know she would be up in arms at my taking a house at all & especially at this time of the year. Last Wednesday I took my mother down to look at the house & of course she raved about it and was sure I should love it so I determined to be as rapid in my movements as possible & prevailed upon Mr Times [solicitor] to go

4. Morgan with his
mother, 1883

with me on Thursday, he also approves in spite of the soil being chalk & loam - the agents said gravel but as usual they lied & I most cleverly found them out. Between you & me I think the situation of the house a cold one, altho' it looks south-west. If I find it cold I shall go away for the winter - don't breathe a word of this at Clapham as they will say I am raving mad to take it. Stevenage is in Herts., about $^3/_4$ hour from Kings Cross, trains run frequently, second class fare 3/7. Mr Times & I saw Col. & Mrs Wilkinson & liked them both very much indeed. His only son was drowned crossing a river during the Zulu War..."

Although Aunt Monie had hoped that Lily and Morgan would stay permanently with her at Clapham, she resigned herself to the fact that they needed to live their own lives. When she was told about Rooksnest, she wrote to Lily;

"Dearest Lily,

This is fine news at last you seem to have killed your fox & from your account you really have got everything that [much mattered to you] except the water but if he'll sink a well that will be all right - the other thing which I am so gregarious that I couldn't stand it, is I believe an inducement to you to take it, that it's away not only from every friend you have but any acquaintance as nearly as possible, like Robinson Crusoe on his desert island!... I know that part of the country, we once stayed with the [...] at a country house they had near Hatfield - it is very pleasant and some parts very pretty... There is so much I want to know. Is the house in the village & how will you do your marketing? How far from the station - what's the return fare & what's the name of your clergyman?... The rent seems wonderfully low for anything so nice as you describe it. Could you hire a good pony chair near - if not you will be [...] to have stables built..."

The move to Rooks Nest was not accomplished until 1883 since, true to her word, Lily spent Christmas at Bournemouth where she had taken a house for the winter. They were there for Morgan's fourth birthday on January 1st and his mother described the day as "quite a carnival." She wrote an account of it to Aunt Monie; "Letter from an eye witness. The happy birthday is over and "Important One " is safe in bed with Dapple Grey... his birthday has been quite a carnival - it began on Sunday morning when Laura's flowers & some presents from Brightstone arrived & today letters cards presents came pouring in from all his admirers..."

Seventy years later Morgan was to write against this description "my earliest memory." In this same letter, his mother reflected over the past year, commenting: "I can hardly believe '82 has gone it seems to have been such an endlessly long year… all my househunting & visits… I shall feel it quite flat when I am really settled at Stevenage for good."

As long as he lived within Aunt Monie's sphere, Morgan was expected to be dressed as she wished. The image of Little Lord Fauntleroy was conjured up by his velvet jackets and long golden curls. He remembered in later years how "I minded… my corkscrew curls. I had to wear these for the old lady's pleasure, and must have been almost the last of the moppets thus to be tormented." Among Aunt Monie's closest friends was the artist George Richmond, one of whose students drew a portrait of Morgan, aged four, dressed in this

5. Rooks Nest. The only extant photograph showing the wych elm, which was felled in the 1960's.

17

fashion. Morgan remarked with acerbity in 1956, "A pupil of Mr Richmond's made a repellent drawing of the curls and of me in their midst."

As winter turned to spring, Lily felt that at last the time had come when she could make arrangements to move into her own house. On 22 February 1883 she received an estimate for £33..10..0 from Chick & Son, Warehousemen, Paddington, to convey furniture thence to Rooksnest and shortly afterwards, in March, she and Morgan set off for a new life.

They travelled by train from Kings Cross, in a second-class carriage. The journey was exciting for Morgan, who was now old enough to read place-names along the route and to ask questions about them. As they passed the village of Welwyn he was surprised that the pronunciation was not as spelled. Here the inspiring viaduct over the River Mimram and the long Welwyn North tunnel impressed themselves upon his memory. He learned later of a tragic accident which had occurred in the tunnel in 1866 when three goods trains collided.

As they approached Stevenage, the railway ran very close to the Great North Road and Morgan saw for the first time that landmark which had been familiar to travellers for at least fifteen hundred years - the row of Roman burial mounds known as the Six Hills. For residents of the town, returning by train from a day in London, they served as a reminder that it was time to collect up bags and parcels, as the train slowed down for the last mile to the station; for travellers by road they had, for centuries, been a welcome sight, marking the outskirts of Stevenage and journey's end. Morgan was immediately fascinated by them, as children always were. Seen from the train window across flat fields, they seemed to dominate the landscape, as indeed the Romans had intended. His curiosity about their origin was to receive a variety of answers, from the local legend that the devil, when digging holes in nearby Whomerley Wood, had tossed over his shoulder six spades of earth which had landed in a neat row beside the road, to the opinion of contemporary historians that they were Danish tumuli. For

18

Morgan, as for all local people, they became a source of pride, a mysterious yet tangible link with the past.

However, the interest of the journey was as nothing compared to Morgan's excitement on his introduction to his new home. The pony and trap which had met them at Stevenage station jolted over the rough road towards Weston. Their view was restricted by high banks on either side, but they did catch the occasional glimpse of undulating ploughed fields through gaps in the hedge. Then they came

upon a farm, and immediately next to it a low brick wall surmounted by iron railings. The pony turned in sharply at a gate on the left and came to a halt outside the front porch of Rooks Nest House.

6. Six Hills, Roman burial mounds on the main road into Stevenage, c. 1900

Morgan was later to recall his immediate and lasting response to Rooks Nest: "The truth is that...I had fallen in love with our Hertfordshire home and did not want to leave it... From the time that I entered the house at the age of four and nearly fell from its top to its bottom through a hole

19

7. Stevenage station c. 1881

ascribed to the mice, I took it to my heart and hoped...that I should live and die there... The impressions received there remain and still glow..."

It is tempting to visualise four-year-old Morgan, dressed in his velvet suit, with his golden ringlets flying, rushing excitedly from room to room. From the hall, dominated by its big ingle-nook fireplace, he could take a door to the left, into the drawing-room, which was large and light, and had attractive French windows into the garden. Or he could turn right, through a little passageway beside the central hearth, and into the dining room, which was smaller and was illuminated by the bay window which they had passed in the pony trap.

At the back of the house, approached by another passage from the hall, was the kitchen, a warm, happy place where a kettle was steaming on the open range. On the ledge above was a collection of candles ready for the night and in the far corner were the six little black bells which connected each of the main rooms to the kitchen, and rang to summon the

20

maids. Opposite the kitchen were the larder and pantry, cool and dim, wherein were several large earthenware vessels containing the entire supply of drinking water for the household. Mrs Forster seems to have accepted the necessity of buying drinking water with equanimity. She also considered that the sanitary arrangements were good, but as these were virtually non-existent save for an earth closet outside the back door it must be supposed that water and drains did not figure high on her list of priorities.

Returning along the passage, Morgan would have seen another door to his right and, on opening it, discovered a

flight of steps leading down to a large cellar beneath the drawing room. Although dark, it had a friendly atmosphere, the curious little niches round the walls giving it the aura of a chapel. This is the oldest part of the house, and some of the original timber framework is incorporated into its walls. From this nucleus, succeeding generations have built on and up during the course of at least four centuries.

8. Servants' bells in the kitchen at Rooks Nest.

For Morgan, in his excited exploration, there remained to investigate one more door in the hall. This, rather unexpectedly, disclosed two narrow flights of stairs which twisted their way to the top of the house. He rushed all the way up to the three attics under the roof, where the maids slept. The central chimney of the house effectively formed the dividing wall between two of the attics, and beside this chimney was a smoking hole, over which the Howards used to hang flitches of bacon. This was the hole "ascribed to the mice" which Morgan remembered all his life as being almost his downfall.

SEARCH FOR
A HOME

9. Stairs to the attics

Safely back on the first floor landing, Morgan would have found the three main bedrooms. The middle one was to be his nursery and from it he could look across the front lawn to neighbouring Rooks Nest Farm, half hidden by a line of elms. There, the rooks whose ancestors had given the hamlet its name were noisily occupied at their nests. Away down the hill, the spire of the parish church was just visible, then the view gradually faded into a blue mist as farmland and woods merged with the distant Chiltern Hills. From the small room at the end of the landing was another lovely view, this time of a meadow, with open country beyond. This room was to be used as a store for apples and preserves, its sweet autumnal scent, mingling with woodsmoke from the open fires, helping to give the house its distinctive and unforgettable aroma.

While Morgan was absorbing the atmosphere of Rooks Nest, his mother was more concerned with the practical matters of furnishing and decoration. Now that they had at last moved in to their own home, she was determined to have it to her own taste and, as she was young and energetic and not at all averse to hard work, alterations were soon noticeable. Unfortunately she appears to have had an unoriginal and rather pernickety approach to interior design, her fussiness about such things as the positioning of furniture and choice of colour resulting in a somewhat uncomfortable atmosphere. She took particular pains with the drawing room, surrounding the fireplace with a large, ornate mantelpiece in dark wood, a feature which dominated the whole room. Once it was completed to her

22

satisfaction she had it photographed by the highly regarded Hitchin photographer, Latchmore, and sent a copy to Aunt Monie, explaining that, apart from what was shown in the picture, "I have 2 little black tea-tables, but since I have had a piano I am obliged to keep them shut up, against the wall - makes no room for them. You only see half the drawing room in the photograph - opposite the fireplace is a tall old-fashioned bureau... and that has a small oak bookcase on each side of it - piano opposite window - you can just see the key of it in the photo..."

The redecoration of Rooks Nest did not always go smoothly. Mrs Forster soon found that the carelessness of a servant or the well-meaning efforts of a country workman could be disastrous. On one occasion she returned from an outing to be greeted by a frantic maid crying, "Such a dreadful thing has happened in your room Ma'am - the register slipped down, and oh, the state of your room." Mrs Forster went upstairs and found that a roaring fire had been burning for two hours with the register [the device for regulating the air flow] tightly shut. The whole room, including the furniture, was "jet black." It took three days to clean up, and even so the walls and paintwork were never the same again.

Some years later, when more redecoration was in progress, Mrs Forster took Morgan to stay with Aunt Monie in Clapham, leaving the house in the hands of the painters. She went back for one day, intending to take down some pictures and empty a wardrobe and was horrified to find that "the man had painted the staircase a most hideous colour. He was supposed to have matched the red paper - the paint was a muddy pink colour... I have made him alter it & have implored him not to do anything awful in the dining room but I tremble."

Living in the country, Mrs Forster and Morgan both noticed that the weather played a much more important part in their lives than it had in London. On calm sunny days they rejoiced in the clear air, uncontaminated by city soot and fog. But in bad weather the house was draughty with great gusts of smoke blowing in at the open fireplaces. In

23

SEARCH FOR A HOME

1883 the spring gales were particularly strong and Rooks Nest, in its hilltop position, caught the full blast. Mrs Forster described it vividly, "The wind is like a fury, howling round the house, slamming doors and shooting the smoke into the room and whirling the dust along the road in a heartrending manner."

She was writing to Aunt Monie, concluding with the wish that she could have got a house nearer her friends. It is unlikely that Aunt Monie was deceived by this, since she had already recognised the younger woman's determination to be independent and self-sufficient. But it is to be hoped that she did not know the true extent of the irritation with her own benevolent interference which Mrs Forster committed to paper on another occasion: "Well well - I hope in the next world there will be a compartment labelled 'Thornton' & that it won't be anywhere near me." So, for all her graphic description, Mrs Forster probably rather enjoyed the feeling of isolation, of being alone with the elements. The wind might roar at her but it could not offer criticism or advice, which must have come as a relief to one who had suffered a surfeit of both. Also, it was clear that country life suited Morgan. His health improved so that his mother was soon referring to "his usual roaring spirits" and dismissing colds and coughs as the minor ailments they were. She was sometimes exasperated because he was so easily moved to tears but Aunt Monie wisely urged her not to take too much notice of this tendency, which she put down to "weak nerves."

Rooks Nest was endlessly fascinating to Morgan, and his affection for it grew as he got to know it intimately. It was a place of unexpected protrusions and uneven floors, where rooms had been added or altered in the past, or where the feet of generations of farmers had worn smooth the original fabric. Yet his obsession with the house did not, apparently, extend to a curiosity about its history. It is inconceivable that local people, or indeed the landlord himself, never referred to the former name of "Howards". The Franklins at the farm next door, the Rector, and not least the servants, are likely to have mentioned the Howards in some context. But they do

24

not appear in any of Mrs Forster's letters and Morgan later claimed never to have heard of them.

It would have been impossible to run a house and grounds the size of Rooks Nest without the aid of servants and - at the period in which the Forsters lived there - unthinkable. The nation was virtually divided into two sectors: those who employed servants and those who were servants, although there were many gradations of both in the social scale. Rooks Nest merited a gardener with one or more boys to assist, a cook and two maids living in, and possibly other domestic help as well. Mrs Forster soon discovered that it was not easy to acquire suitable servants, nor to keep them once she had found them. The position of Rooks Nest, separated by one and a half miles of rough road from Stevenage, which was itself no more than a large village, was unattractive to many young people. Moreover, since good servants were very much sought after, Mrs

10. The hall at Rooks Nest when the Forsters lived there.

Forster was in competition with others of her class.

As a newcomer to the district, Mrs Forster was not at first aware of the accepted local rates for servants, and it was not long before she was taken to task about this by her neighbour, Mrs Franklin. She reported to Aunt Monie, "I find that wages in the country are much less than I gave & Mrs Franklyn [sic] hoped I would not think her inquisitive but her maid told her I gave £20 to Lina & she knew it was not true & wished me to confirm her . I said it was true." Once she realised that £20 per year was excessive, Mrs Forster decided to keep the unfortunate Lina for only another month and then to take on a replacement, paying her "much less wages."

One or two of the girls who worked for Mrs Forster were very young indeed, probably not much more than ten years old, which was then the official school leaving age. They were certainly young enough to enjoy playing with Morgan, but sadly for all concerned it soon became obvious that their general knowledge could not compare with his. Thus it came about that a child of five began to instruct girls of twice, perhaps three times, his age in such subjects as geography, astronomy and dancing. Emma Dickens, who worked for Mrs Forster for several years and became a good friend to Morgan, was one of his first "pupils." She threw herself with enthusiasm into his dancing lessons, in which he endeavoured to teach her the polka, a dance he had recently learnt from his mother. Mrs Forster observed wryly that Emma was "but a sorry dancer - heavy-footed, for the drawing room windows and doors rattle and the furniture screams." Then the dancers would shake tambourines and play musical boxes, at the same time shouting at the tops of their voices. Mrs Forster showed considerable forbearance while this was going on, merely remarking that her afternoons were lively.

When it came to academic subjects however, the gulf between "pupil" and "teacher" was insurmountable. The maids were not at all interested in studying the heavens and poor Emma was reprimanded for calling the planet Jupiter a star. She enjoyed the more active lessons and liked drawing

26

with coloured chalks, but soon lost concentration when Morgan tried to make her study an atlas or learn chess. Reluctantly he admitted defeat, and asked his mother to help him draw a map of South America, telling her, "I know Emma won't think it matters a bit whether I put Patagonia in the place of Ecuador." In a mournful, resigned manner, he said at another time, "Mamma, it is a pity that Emma has so little sense." Mrs Forster may have secretly agreed with this, since it was Emma who left the roaring fire burning in her bedroom, thereby causing so much damage. In spite of Emma's much criticised frivolity and apparent ignorance, she was an ideal companion in other ways. She and Morgan often played hide-and-seek, a game for which the house was well-suited, and as he squeezed into cupboards or hunted behind curtains, Morgan got to know every corner of his home.

But when the games were over, the gulf between "the little master" and the maid was as great as ever. The class divide which separated them was as powerful as the patriotism which divided the nations. Indeed, Morgan and Emma might almost have belonged to two different races; he the cosseted child of a wealthy and cultured family, she from a cramped cottage, where there was no time or money for anything but the bare necessities of existence. Compulsory education had been introduced only a few years before and was still resented by some village families who relied on their children to help with the harvest and other seasonal jobs. School attendance was sometimes difficult to enforce and a high level of academic attainment was not expected, since the vast majority of girls would go into domestic service and the boys to work on the land. For many children the local craft of straw-plaiting was an accomplishment which was more important than book-learning. For years many Stevenage families had depended for part of their income on straw plait, made mainly by women and children, and sold to hat manufacturers for the production of straw hats. This trade had dwindled by the end of the nineteenth century, but was still flourishing while the Forsters were at

Rooks Nest. Phoebe, one of their maids, was an accomplished straw-plaiter.

Although Emma was an exception, most of the Rooks Nest maids came and went with annoying rapidity, and their replacement took up a good deal of Mrs Forster's time. She may well have used the services of the *Stevenage Local Magazine* which, in January 1884, announced:

Registry for Servants

"It has been suggested to us by several ladies that the magazine might be made useful as a medium of communication between mistresses and servants. We therefore have made arrangements to insert advertisements from mistresses requiring servants and servants seeking situations, at a uniform charge of 1/-.

Servants sending advertisements must enclose a recommendation from the clergyman of, or some lady in, the parish in which they reside, as a guarantee of respectability."

Whatever means she used, searching for servants was not an exercise Mrs Forster enjoyed. She wrote wearily to Maimie, "I have a new housemaid coming on 23rd, may her reign be long and uneventful."

As regards cooking, Mrs Forster discovered that she herself was quite a good cook and soon her culinary skill reached such heights as to make Aunt Monie exclaim, "I stand astonished at your successful cooking. Roll puddings I think I could make, but the Irish stew is quite beyond me." She also became interested in making jam and marmalade, and took to exchanging recipes with her family. Laura Forster, her husband's sister, sent a new recipe for marmalade, and she duly reported the results: "Good marmalade from your recipe - the first lot had too much water and had to be boiled an hour too long to make its jelly - but I cut off 1 quart of water in the second lot as I put two pounds less sugar in mine and the smaller quantity of water made all the difference, it is a splendid colour and consistency."

She then added the information that Morgan said he was about to be sick, but whether from tasting the marmalade is not clear. Making preserves from home-grown fruit was very satisfying. Apples, pears and cherries were abundant in the Rooks Nest garden, and one year the pear tree bore so well that mother and son spent four hours picking the fruit and filling wicker clothes-baskets with it. Aunt Laura, who was staying with them at the time had some difficulty in making her way through the hall, it was so cluttered with produce.

Although she enjoyed cooking, Mrs Forster had no intention of taking it on permanently and she tried to ensure that she

11. Apples and jug

always had either a cook or a maid who could help in the kitchen. Cooks were more difficult to come by than maids, so she sometimes had to go by train to the county town of Hertford, where there was an agency for domestic servants. But none of the Rooks Nest cooks stayed very long, probably because of the loneliness of a house which was well away from the town and too small to maintain a large enough staff of servants to provide a lively social life.

Now that she was free to organise her life as she chose, Mrs Forster turned for support and companionship to her own family, the Whichelos. Her mother, known to Morgan as "Gran", was a frequent and delightful visitor. She liked Rooks Nest and had thoroughly supported her daughter's decision to take the house. On her first visit, soon after they had moved in, Morgan excitedly showed her round, "doing the honours" and taking her up to her room. "I do hope you will be comfortable, Grandmama," he said, "but I am afraid you will be bothered by flies, as we have a great many." Fortunately Mrs Whichelo was "charmed" by the house and its surroundings, and enjoyed her stay. She was a cheerful, lovable woman and Morgan was always happy in her company. Accustomed to dealing with children after bringing up ten of her own, she had the knack of letting him

29

enjoy himself without getting too excited. Of all his relations she was perhaps the most relaxed and dependable.

While Morgan was worrying about flies, Mrs Forster had another visitor to contend with, as she later informed Aunt Monie "I was awake from 1 to 6 on Tuesday with a mouse in my room. I had to fetch the cat & she sat with me most of the night & I was thankful when she caught the mouse at 6.0. I am not afraid of mice but after seeing it on my bed & crawling up baby's pillow I really couldn't take things easily." In view of the age of the house, and the attractions of the store room next to the bedroom, this visitation was not surprising. The maids in their attics probably had mouse visitors every night, as some of the original thatch of the roof was still intact under its later covering of tiles, furnishing ideal nesting places for a variety of creatures.

From time to time other Whichelos came to stay, including Mrs Forster's lively and pretty sister Rosie, whom Morgan thought very attractive; her younger brother Harry and her nephew Percy, who was a few years older than Morgan. The affection of her own family was a consolation to Mrs Forster in the loneliness of her widowhood, and a source of warmth and security for Morgan.

As far as her husband's family was concerned, Mrs Forster maintained close links with some, but was content to keep others at a distance. She was in continuous correspondence with Aunt Monie, and stayed at her Clapham house several times each year, visits she later came to dread. Maimie Synnot remained her closest friend and *confidante*. She was a frequent visitor to Rooks Nest, her only fault being her inability to be firm with Morgan. She was kind and gentle and he loved her very much, but all too often he would show off in front of her and indulge in his "stupid habit of throwing things down for no reason in the world." Mrs Forster said in exasperation that Maimie made him behave like an idiot, but that was her way with all children. However, the bond between the two women was strong enough to withstand these temporary embarrassments, and they sometimes managed to take a day out together away from Morgan's demanding presence.

30

Morgan was always miserable once their guests had left. After one of Maimie's visits he was quite disconsolate, telling his mother, "I keep stretching out my hand to her and she is not there." But he decided to go up to her room after all, because "Perhaps by chance she might have come back." He went upstairs and stamped around the deserted room, then came down expecting his mother to be surprised when he told her that Maimie had gone. Visits from his relations always left Morgan unsettled for a time, as he had to adjust from taking part in adult conversation to playing simple country games with the domestic servants. Although he did not realise it, Morgan was lonely.

12. Kitchen doors at Rooks Nest

2
NEIGHBOURS

Loneliness, to a greater or lesser extent, is inevitable for most only children. In the class-conscious 1880's and 90's fraternisation between children of different backgrounds was usually frowned upon, and true friendship between them was a rare occurrence. Thus Morgan was doubly isolated at Rooks Nest; he had no brothers or sisters to share his delightful new home, nor were there any young people of his own class nearby. His mother displayed a curiously ambivalent attitude in this respect. She did not mind, indeed even encouraged, his friendship with the young servants, but she herself made very little attempt to socialise locally. After the sophisticated circle she had been accustomed to mix with in London, Stevenage must have seemed very provincial. She appears to have deemed the majority of her rural neighbours inferior in both social standing and culture, and to have used the railway as her lifeline to the capital when she felt in need of society.

Through necessity or propinquity, Mrs Forster had to establish relationships with some of her neighbours. The least avoidable of these was Colonel Robert Hindley Wilkinson, owner of Chesfield Park and landlord of Rooks Nest. When she first met him, Mrs Forster was impressed by his tall figure and striking appearance, and told her family that she liked him and his wife very much indeed. He was an acquaintance of Ruthven Pym, her husband's cousin by marriage, and when Aunt Monie heard this she wrote approvingly, "Ruthven knows your landlord very well indeed...I am glad to know him to be respectable as you are to be such near neighbours." But Mrs Forster remarked with some asperity to Maimie, "I long to retort that I don't see why Mr Pym's knowing him should stamp him as respectable."

Colonel Wilkinson paid several visits to his new tenant during her first year. Unfortunately Morgan took a dislike to him. When the Colonel pulled teasingly at Morgan's curls, there was an outburst of screaming and bad temper. The Important One was not used to rough handling, or even to the kind of jovial teasing that fathers, uncles or grandfathers often indulge in. Mrs Forster took some pains to explain to him that it was prudent to be pleasant to one's landlord, particularly as there was a number of repairs that needed doing. On the Colonel's next visit, Morgan was a model of politeness, as his relieved mother told Aunt Monie:

> "Col. Wilkinson came to see me yesterday about some cracked doors and parquet blocks of which [sic] are loose. M. was very good and quiet and only spoke three times, first to beg Col. W. to take ' a more comfortable chair', 2nd to say 'hadn't you better show Col.W. the nursery door it squeaks dreadfully - wants a little oil '- he accompanied us to the dining room and began taking up all the blocks so Col. W. saw I had not exaggerated & 3rdly just as Col. W. was going out of the front door M. ran forward with a tangerine in his hand -'I only want to say one thing Mamma - I thought Col. W. would like an orange.' His face was quite pink as he placed the orange in Col. W's hand, M. looking such a mite by the side of Col. W. who looks like a giant. Col.W. seemed much gratified & said he would eat the orange after his dinner. I am so glad M. was so agreeable..."

Colonel Wilkinson's visits soon became very infrequent, making it difficult for Mrs Forster to discuss household matters with him. At first this was just a cause of mild annoyance and some amusement. Replying to a letter from Aunt Monie, she asked, "How did you know I received Col. W. in my hat, but you are quite right I did. If you think wearing a bonnet would make all the difference in his behaviour to me I must certainly dawdle about the garden in one, hoping he may call, I have seen no more of him..." Mrs Forster's amusement faded as it became clear that Colonel Wilkinson was deliberately avoiding her. One Sunday he passed her in his carriage as she was walking down the muddy road to church and bowed low, but did not stop. As a newcomer, alone, she had no pew reserved for her use and so sat in the "free"seats with "a row of gazing, snuffling, dirty girls in front of me." She was a little mollified to walk back with Caroline and Charles Poyntz-Stewart, Colonel Wilkinson's daughter and son-in-law, who were complaining because Mrs Wilkinson's illness obliged them to stay at Chesfield. Mr Poyntz-Stewart confided that his mother-in-law was very irritable, and Mrs Forster concluded that he was having a bad time, with both the Wilkinsons in "such an awful humour."

As time went on, relations between landlord and tenant deteriorated badly. The water supply was a contentious issue between them, Colonel Wilkinson having delayed the provision of a well at Rooks Nest for several years. His apparently unreasonable obstinacy may have been in part a reaction to Mrs Forster's manner, which could be very sharp and insistent, not showing the subservience due from tenant - and female tenant in particular - to landlord. Perhaps there were faults on both sides, but Mrs Forster's position was the more vulnerable, and after one unpleasant episode she gave way to tears. Aunt Monie was very upset to hear of this, and wrote anxiously, "Do you know your last letter (the one on striped sheets of paper) made me quite unhappy about you - you seemed so unprotected and the idea of you being insulted and made to cry almost made me cry too..." She could not refrain from reminding Mrs Forster of the folly of living in such an isolated place, away from everyone she knew, but went on to commiserate with her, saying that, "A lone woman (or rather girl) is no match for a ponderous owner of a domain - and tho' it's strange still it's true that the more you are right in any dispute with him the more angry he will be. In this badly put together world might is the only right that prevails in the long run especially where women are concerned..."

Colonel Wilkinson had troubles of his own, as the Poyntz-Stewarts had indicated. His elder son had died while still a child and his younger son, Edward, by all accounts a charming and courageous young man, was killed in heroic circumstances while helping wounded colleagues to safety across the Ingogo River during the Zulu War in Africa. Mrs Wilkinson was an invalid and not a very patient one. Consequently his daughter and son-in-law had to spend much of their time at Chesfield, a duty which they did not enjoy in view of the prevalent atmosphere of gloom. In 1884

34

the birth of Niel [sic], the Poyntz-Stewarts' son and the Wilkinsons' only grandchild, brought consolation to the family, but after a while solace turned to anxiety as they became concerned about the slowness of his mental development. Colonel Wilkinson continued to fulfil the role expected of him in the community; he was a JP, a member of numerous committees and a benefactor of local charities. But none of this made up to Mrs Forster for the distress and annoyance he had caused her, nor did Morgan overcome his dislike of the man who made his mother so unhappy. Landlords were to remain in his memory as an unpleasant species of humanity.

At first, Mrs Forster thought the Poyntz-Stewarts pleasant enough, on the few occasions when she met them. But as Charles Poyntz-Stewart took a greater part in the management of the Chesfield estate, she began to find him pompous and overbearing. In 1888 Colonel Wilkinson died, leaving his property to his daughter. Charles Poyntz-Stewart visited the Rooks Nest tenants on her behalf and made the great mistake of coupling the Franklins with Mrs Forster. She reminded him in no uncertain terms that the Forsters were not to be spoken of in the same breath as their farming neighbours, writing indignantly to tell her mother about the incident. Mrs Whichelo replied comfortingly that she had been quite right. "I am glad you chaffed and chafed Mr Poyntz-S. I never heard such want of tact - to couple you with Mr Franklin...Little men are all the same. I have said so from my birth. The pomposity and 'ponderosity' of some one I could name! The word in inverted commas is my own - good is it not?"

Although his mother looked down on the Franklins of Rooks Nest Farm, Morgan found them far more congenial than their domineering Chesfield neighbours. Philip Franklin, the farmer, was kind to children and tolerated Morgan and his own grandson, Frank, playing in the farmyard, running in and out of the barns and even jumping into his straw ricks. The Franklins also had several young daughters and they were happy, cheerful girls, who welcomed lonely little Morgan into their midst. Mrs

35

NEIGHBOURS

Franklin had a countrywoman's wisdom and a deep knowledge of local lore, and Morgan was much impressed by her. Visits to the farm became important in his life.

Philip Franklin took a considerable part in the affairs of local government. For many years he was a member of the Stevenage Local Board, as the fore-runners of district councils were known. He had a cautious approach to public expenditure; the poor state of the footpaths in Stevenage was a permanent cause for concern at meetings, but Philip Franklin was of the opinion that "The Board must be careful not to spend too much money." There were other branches of the Franklin family in the district, including Thomas Franklin, well-known corn and coal merchant, and staunch supporter of the Liberal party. They tended to be too blunt and down to earth for Mrs Forster, who was highly embarrassed on one occasion when she met "Old Franklin." Pointing towards his niece, who happened to be passing on the other side of the road, he said she had two children already and he thought she was fairly on the way to a third, adding that he had not been told about it, but judged by the look of her. "Horrid old man!" exclaimed Mrs Forster later. "I should have liked to have tipped him into the horse pond."

Although she condescended to the Franklins, Mrs Forster was glad enough of their presence in an emergency. A rather bizarre episode, which caused temporary chaos at Rooks Nest, was the arrival of two men with a performing bear. Mrs Forster was out when they came, but the maid saw them through a window and refused to open the door. The men then retreated to a haystack, where they spent the night sheltering from a howling blizzard. By morning, when Mrs Forster looked cautiously out, the bear had escaped and the men were searching frantically for it. Bible, the Forsters' garden boy, was called, but did not hear. When the Franklins rallied their men to the rescue the shepherd ran away in terror, insisting that a wild animal was after him. Meanwhile, unaware of the panic, young Frank was walking along the road when he heard footsteps and, turning round, came face to face with the bear, an incident he remembered

36

vividly all his life and related to his children and grandchildren. Eventually Tom Franklin and the keeper managed to round up both men and bear and escorted them to the police station by the Bowling Green, whence they were escorted from the town.

"What's the name of your clergyman?" had been one of Aunt Monie's first questions when she was told about the move to Rooks Nest. Quite soon Mrs Forster was able to tell her a good deal about the Rector of Stevenage, the Reverend William Jowitt, because rather surprisingly she became friendly with his wife Louisa. The Rector was a warm-hearted, jovial man, who enjoyed outdoor activities such as hunting. He took a full part in the life of Stevenage, being chairman of almost every board and committee and always present at public functions. He was well-supported in his work by his wife, who took the responsibilities of her position very seriously, and also by his nine daughters, who were brought up to serve the community. His only son, William, born in 1885, was too young to provide Morgan with the companionship he longed for and the two never became close friends.

13. The Reverend William Jowitt, Rector of Stevenage 1874 - 1912

The Rector was popular in his parish. His sermons and public speeches were not always of the highest academic level, but no one minded as his words at least had the merit of being delivered in loud ringing tones, so that even the hard of hearing could understand him. Most

14. St Nicholas' Church

of the village children respected and admired the Rector, but Morgan realised that his sermons often lacked clarity and privately he tended to be rather critical. Mrs Forster was, as a matter of course, bringing up her son in the Anglican tradition of the Christian faith, and Morgan listened to Bible stories and tales about missionaries with the same eagerness that he showed for all knowledge. He even had daydreams in which he imagined himself converting the inhabitants of New Guinea to Christianity. As soon as he was old enough his mother had begun taking him to services, as she told Maimie in a note scrawled across the top of one letter:

"Baby is going to church with me this afternoon." As a child, Morgan accepted the religious teachings of his mother and his aunts, and sincerely tried to live up to them. But when he was in one of his furious rages he forgot everything, and flung his mother's hymn and prayer books across the room, much to her annoyance.

Mrs Forster's friendship with Mrs Jowitt prevented her from withdrawing entirely from the society of the neighbourhood, but it was some time before the Rector's wife managed to involve her a little in "visiting the women." This was an age when the poor were very poor, often inhabiting crowded, insanitary cottages, such as those in Back Lane (now known as Church Lane). The women of these families could be hard put to it to feed and clothe their children even in the comparatively good times. When illness struck, or when there was no employment for their husbands, life became a grim struggle for survival. Help from the Church, or from philanthropic individuals, might take the form of food, second-hand clothes, or other necessities of life. There were also attempts to provide basic

38

education in hygiene, child-care and domestic economy.
Activities such as sewing circles had the dual functions of
practical training and companionship. Many of the wealthy
families in the district were deeply concerned for the welfare
of their social inferiors although, in keeping with the spirit
of the age, the majority had no will for radical change,
accepting the unequal distribution of poverty and riches as a
fact of life.

Mrs Jowitt, as the Rector's wife, saw it as her Christian

duty to take the lead in ministering to the poor. Mrs Forster's
social conscience was not so highly developed, but she
followed Mrs Jowitt's lead in these matters and came to place
a certain reliance on her advice. Unfortunately, when this
new friend was introduced to Maimie the two did not get on
at all well, so Mrs Jowitt made a point of keeping away from
Rooks Nest when Maimie was staying there.

15. Stevenage Rectory, with the Rector and Mrs Jowitt

NEIGHBOURS   The Jowitt family lived at the Rectory in Rectory Lane, the road which led down from St Nicholas' Church to join the Great North road at the point where a tollgate for the turnpike road had once stood. At this lower end of Rectory Lane was Woodfield, a substantial property which had its origins in the sixteenth century or even earlier. It had formerly belonged to the Church and its large grounds adjoined the probable site of mediaeval religious buildings. Woodfield was owned by Rear-Admiral Butler Fellowes, C.B. and his wife Constance. She was one of those who was concerned for the poor women of Back Lane, and with the help of her husband, who built a Public Room for them, she ran a mothers' meeting there for many years. The genuine kindness of Admiral and Mrs Fellowes, and of others like them, made an immense contribution to the life of Stevenage. Class divisions were so entrenched, so much a part of the fabric of society, that they were virtually never questioned.

Some seventy years later, reflecting on his life at Rooks Nest, Morgan wrote: "Part of the trouble was that there were too few children in our lovely retreat. At the park gate dwelt Baby Plum Bun or Sizzle, of inferior lineage and age...Down in the Rectory were nine daughters, to whom was presently added a future Lord Chancellor. And there were a few more children in the village..." The "Baby Plum Bun" referred to here was the son of Mr Plum, gamekeeper, and his wife, who lived at the south lodge of Chesfield Park, a little further up the lane from Rooks Nest. As a child Morgan disliked the Plums and so, apparently, did his mother. Their antipathy seems to have been more than a little tinged with superiority as they indulged in the Victorian sport of making fun of the mispronunciations of the lower orders. "Sizzle" (Cecil) and his sister "Littlannie" stuck in Morgan's mind and reappeared many years later in another guise. His reference to "a few more children in the village" is also indicative of the way in which individuals were prisoners of their class. During the years that the Forsters lived there, the population of Stevenage included a good percentage of children. The "few" to whom Morgan referred were those of his own class.

40

But even in the socially restrictive days of his childhood he did attempt to break through barriers, just as in his novels he would try, not always convincingly, to reconcile characters from different backgrounds.

About a mile to the south east of Rooks Nest, on Pin Green hill, was another tiny hamlet called Highfield, consisting of a Georgian mansion with a few cottages. The Hitchin auctioneer, George Jackson, described it as:

> "RESIDENCE, standing in its own grounds on an eminence, commanding extensive views over the surrounding country, and approached from the road by a carriage drive with large lawn tennis ground, kitchen and pleasure gardens, conservatory; hot-house, etc; excellent stabling for four horses; carriage house and other outbuildings; about 13 acres of grass land, with use of two or three cows, horse and phaeton; gardener, coachman and cowman; one maidservant will remain on the premises. The house contains 7 bedrooms and dressing room, cheerful drawing room, dining room, library or morning room, dairy, kitchen and domestic offices; good supply of hard and soft water."

When the Forsters came to Stevenage in 1883, Highfield was occupied by Mr George Salmon, who moved away in 1886. The property was subsequently taken by Charles Poston, a stockbroker. He had been born in Romford but went to London as a young man, where he made a very successful

16. Entrance drive to Highfield

NEIGHBOURS

career in the City. He was now married with a teenage son, young Charles, and a daughter, May, who was slightly older.

The Poston family were quickly assimilated into the life of Stevenage. Charles and Rector Jowitt had many interests in common, and they formed a friendship which was to last for the rest of their lives. Mrs Poston and May were soon caught up in Mrs Jowitt's parish work and, of course, were introduced to the Forsters. This was the beginning of a much more sociable period in Mrs Forster's life, in which she paid calls with Mrs Jowitt, exchanged visits with the Postons and joined in their tennis parties and other enjoyable recreations. Charles was kind and avuncular to Morgan while May, by all accounts a particularly sweet-natured young woman, was a great favourite of both Morgan and his mother.

Once they had settled in, the Postons began to make alterations and improvements to Highfield. This was something after Mrs Forster's heart and she watched the changes with interest, noting the addition of a billiard room, kitchen and extra bedroom and a new bay window for May's room, to match the one in the morning room below. She and Mrs Poston spent many a pleasant afternoon discussing furnishings and colour schemes. During one of their conversations, May told Mrs Forster that her father had decided to keep the family carriage in London, where it would be driven by their present coachman, Slow. The man's erratic driving was notorious, and Mrs Forster was horrified at the thought of his trying to control his horses in the crowded streets of London. She tried tactfully to point out the dangers of this plan, declaring that the Postons would not live to enjoy the improvements to their home. May dismissed her fears, saying cheerfully: "Oh yes, we all know he drives badly, but father will have him up and he is to drive about alone for some time to find places." "Bless the child," said Mrs Forster, "it isn't places he will find but things for he will certainly be smashed but I trust he will be smashed alone." Her fears were unfounded and the Postons continued to entrust their lives to Slow.

Morgan often went to Highfield with his mother. The Postons always struck him as full of confidence and energy

42

with an outgoing attitude to life which was somewhat different to anything he had encountered so far in his own restricted environment. Charles Poston was often away in London but when at home he and his son spent a great deal of their time in outdoor sporting activities. At such times, Highfield seemed full of hearty, cheerful beings, secure in their position in society, untroubled by doubts. Nor did the Postons keep their good fortune to themselves. The whole family played its part in local affairs, even the youngest. The *Stevenage Local Magazine* for September 1889, reporting on the success of a sale of work to raise money for an organ for Holy Trinity Church, solemnly recorded that stall *vii* raised £5..19..9 and that one of the stall-holders was Master Poston.

So life went on in Stevenage, uneventful by London standards, but not without its local excitements, and Morgan and his mother were drawn a little into it, thanks largely to the Jowitts and the Postons. For those with an interest in the vagaries of human nature, the district was as full of colourful figures as any other: James Flack, John Bailey Denton, the Revd. John Lingen Seager, the Warner Smiths of Stevenage Bury, the notorious twin poachers Albert and Ebenezer Fox were but a few of those who contributed in their various ways to the character of the town. But Mrs Forster never quite became assimilated into local life; there was always a distance between her and her new neighbours. Rooks Nest was now her home, but the people of Stevenage remained acquaintances.

17. Stevenage High Street, c. 1910

3
DIVERSIONS

The Forsters had moved into Rooks Nest as winter was coming to an end and during the following weeks Morgan had experienced his first country spring. As the weather improved he was allowed to spend more time out of doors, well wrapped up in deference to his supposedly delicate constitution. The sounds and smells of the garden must have been almost overwhelming at first to a city child unused to outdoor life. It was the air which immediately impinged on his senses; it smelled clean and its breeze was cool as it touched his face, bringing faint colour into his cheeks, teasing him with mingled scents of wet earth, bonfire smoke, damp leaves and new growth. When a spring gale blew through the garden, making the trees roar like waves of the sea, Mrs Forster would anxiously call Morgan indoors in case the wind brought on one of his coughs and, reluctantly, he would turn his back on his exciting new playground.

The front garden of Rooks Nest consisted mainly of a large lawn sloping down to the hedge which separated them from the Farm. Between the lawn and the hedge was a boggy depression known as the dell-'ole or "dellow." There were narrow flower beds and borders on either side of the lawn and under the front windows of the house. A driveway ran straight past the front of the house, between it and the lawn, leading to the stables and paddock at the back, at one point skirting a large tree which at first glance did not appear particularly interesting. On closer examination, Morgan was surprised to find some pigs' teeth embedded in the bark. Mrs Forster was equally puzzled and could throw no light on the matter beyond establishing that the tree was a wych elm. Later they were told by local people of a belief that toothache in humans could be cured if a pig's tooth were stuck into wych elm bark.

At the back of the house was a vegetable garden and some fruit trees. A grass path ran between these, into a small shrubbery and then on round to the orchard, which merged into the boundary hedge. Apart from the garden itself, Mrs Forster also rented the two fields which went with the house, one of which she kept for her own pony while the other was let to Mr Franklin at the farm next door, for grazing. There was plenty of space for Morgan to play in, but no brothers or sisters to join him in childish games. Realising that her son needed companionship, Mrs Forster arranged for successive garden boys to play with him on Wednesday afternoons. The garden boys, like the housemaids, were mostly very young and none of them stayed long. Their work was to help the gardener, to tend the pony and to do odd jobs such as fetching the coal. Young Wray was one of the first of Morgan's playmates and the two got on so well together that the maids were relegated to second place. Morgan now only asked them to tea with him on Sundays, when Wray had the day off. Mrs Forster was apparently quite happy about the friendship, but her mother, Mrs Whichelo, disagreed. While staying at Rooks Nest she formed a poor opinion of Wray, telling her daughter, "Wray is a silently impudent boy I think and awfully idle - but as I said before is respectable and not swarming with vermin, which is the rule with country people I believe and thought

18. The kitchen garden at Rooks Nest, with Mrs Forster and her nephew, Herbert Whichelo

no disgrace." Unaware of his grandmother's strictures, Morgan continued to enjoy life in the open air with his new companion and his health improved noticeably, though he was still subject to frequent coughs and colds, which his mother treated very seriously, often keeping him indoors longer than was strictly necessary. But she had to admit that this did not suit him, and she told Aunt Monie, "He does not eat as well when he stays indoors."

After Wray there was a succession of garden boys, including Chalkley, Taylor and Bible, all local names. The Bible family was well-known in the neighbourhood. Mr S. Bible was organist at Graveley Church and a founder member of the Stevenage Football Club. Edward, the Rooks Nest Bible, was a chorister and a cricket enthusiast, while his little sister Nettie achieved local fame with her recital of a monologue entitled *The Dead Doll* at one annual tea of of the Church of England Temperance Society. Edward was not always as efficient as Mrs Forster would have liked. He had been known to go off at night without filling the coal scuttles, leaving Mrs Forster and the maids to manage as best they could. His reactions to other people's ideas were unpredictable, so that when a visitor took it upon herself to make a blue string cap for the pony without consulting him, Mrs Forster was a little nervous. Fortunately, Bible was quite pleased, giving as his verdict that the pony looked very nice.

Inevitably the time came when Bible, too, decided to leave and once again Mrs Forster was faced with a recruitment problem. Then Bible changed his mind and said he would stay on a little longer, for which reprieve Mrs Forster was grateful, though no doubt irritated that these matters were not more within her own control.

Of all the boys who worked at Rooks Nest, Morgan's favourite was Ansell. He, also, came from a large family and had many uncles, aunts and cousins living in and around Stevenage. Morgan found his strong Hertfordshire accent amusing at first, but lost his smug superiority as his respect for the older boy increased. Ansell was more of a thinker than the other garden boys had been, and although his education was no better than theirs, his mind was more in tune with Morgan's. From him, Morgan learned a new perspective on life, the dim realisation that there was another world outside his own; a world of material insecurity and of dependence on the whims of one's "betters." Yet he was also aware that the garden boy had what he lacked: Ansell had his roots in Stevenage; he belonged, he had no doubts about his status. Morgan was a stranger and no matter how kind Ansell was, Morgan could never be truly a part of his fraternity. Furthermore, as a result of his mother's withdrawal from the society of most of her own class, there too, Morgan was cut off from friendship. His only certainty was Rooks Nest, and here, for the time being, he was secure. Intimations of another life beyond the bounds of his own home came only fleetingly and for the most part he was carefree and happy, especially on Wednesday afternoons when, he recalled later, "My mother in her kindness let Ansell off...so that he could play with me. We mostly played on a straw-rick which Mr Franklin abandoned to our fury. More kindness. We slid and we shouted. Ansell hid and left his billycock as a decoy. Not finding him I jumped on it and stove it in, and this did ruffle him. Once we built a hut between the rick and the hedge...We stored apples there and could not think what ate them."

Morgan never forgot Ansell and the comradeship they shared in their Hertfordshire youth. In *The Longest Journey*, Morgan's semi-autobiographical novel published in 1907, the enigmatic character Stewart Ansell, a scholar of humble origins, acts almost as a guardian angel to Ricky, the character who has so much in common with Morgan himself.

Another tribute to his childhood companion, written in 1903 but unpublished until 1972, is Morgan's story *Ansell*. It is very short and, superficially at least, very simple. It centres round the reunion after several years of the highly-educated narrator and his childhood friend, the former garden-boy now gamekeeper, Ansell. Although the plot is fictitious, the story includes passages which are nothing less than Morgan's reminiscences of Ansell at Rooks Nest:

DIVERSIONS

"We scraped out a hole in the side of the large straw stack, and made it into a house, where we stored apples and gooseberries and 'Kola' lemonade, which we got cheap from Ansell's aunt in the village. We made birdlime from a recipe in *The Boys' Own Book*, and caught Mrs Perill's prize bantam chickens in it. The sound of our whoops and shrieks as we jumped with abandon on one another's hats penetrated even into the smoking room..."

Pleased that Morgan was responding so well to the benefits of country life, Mrs Forster turned her attention to the garden. When she had first inspected Rooks Nest one of its attractions for her had been the amount of land that went with it and she had talked enthusiastically about making a garden. Now she set about putting her plans into operation, undertaking much of the work on the flower-beds herself. She decided to fill up the wet dell-'ole at the end of the lawn to provide space for a shrubbery underplanted with spring bulbs. This project was never completed, although she did make a start by planting rambler roses and dozens of tulips. The result was very pleasing so that in the spring she remarked on "My tulips blazing away in their glory." Roses followed the tulips, usually blooming throughout the summer and well into the autumn. Even in winter the dell-'ole was attractive under a carpet of snowdrops but the ground always remained rather squelchy, especially after rain. Morgan loved the dell-'ole, sometimes wishing they had made it into a water garden. Ever since he and Emma had come across a pond not far from the house, he had been interested in water creatures, but had to be satisfied with an aquarium, as he told Maimie: "...do you know we have an aquarium and some tadpoles and water-snails in it."

As roses were particular favourites of Mrs Forster, she put a great many in the borders, anxiously watching their progress. It annoyed her that her family - Aunt Monie in particular - expected her to pay them extended visits just when the garden was beginning to repay her hard work. She wrote to Maimie from Aunt Monie's house in Clapham: "I do so want to be at home this year and have my friends and enjoy my garden." Morgan fully agreed with her. He did not like leaving Rooks Nest at any time, but he especially disliked Clapham, saying, "The sun never seems to shine

48

here - the room gets lighter or darker, but he never throws his rays in as he does at home." Much as he disliked her house, Morgan was fond of Aunt Monie and grateful for her kindness to him. One of her gifts, when he was very small, had been a gardener's apron: "I send you a gardener's apron for working in the garden, nothing will improve your appetite like being a gardener, and so intelligent as you are you will soon be...head man." Whether or not Morgan's enthusiasm matched Aunt Monie's has not been recorded, but he certainly had his own patch of garden near the back door, where he grew tall red poppies.

The garden at Rooks Nest was a natural haven for birds; their songs filled the air. Little flocks of finches and tomtits flitted lightly through the trees, doves had taken possession of the roof-tops and there were always the rooks cawing in the background. One great attraction was the abundance of fruit. Raspberry canes, gooseberry and currant bushes could be protected from hungry beaks by means of nets or wire cages, but trees were more difficult to deal with. When Mrs Forster's younger brother, Harry Whichelo, was staying with her, he devised a plan to deter the birds from attacking a large cherry near the kitchen. Climbing the tree, he placed four hats in strategic positions, where he thought they would cause most alarm to winged invaders. Then he hung a bell from a high branch, and attached to it a long rope, which reached to the landing window. "Every time we go upstairs we ring the bell," said Mrs Forster. "I hope the pleasure of eating cherries will repay us." Morgan thought the idea a splendid one and rang the bell vigorously as often as he could. He was disillusioned fairly soon by a blackbird which, perched placidly on the bell, surveyed the hats with interest.

Not all birds were after the fruit, however. Mrs Forster was intrigued one morning to see a wren hop in at her window. It had probably nested in the vine which covered the front wall of the house, and become quite tame. It seemed unafraid of the human occupants of Rooks Nest. Apart from cats and the occasional fox, birds had no enemies here; pheasants and partridges often wandered in, strolling happily along the grass paths, followed by large families of squeaking infants. Poultry and assorted animals belonging to the Franklins came in through the thin hedges and fences dividing the properties, making the garden look like an extension of the farmyard. Morgan recollected later that:

> "The garden was always overrun with animals... There were always hens and guinea-fowls. These we were used to, but also there was always a sample of whatever animal happened to be in the meadow. If it was large it crashed through by the dell, if small it crawled under the bottom wire of the fence. To the former class belonged cows, calves and sheep, to the latter pigs, lambs, hens, ducks and guinea-fowls. Add to these the occasional animals that strayed in from the road and the keeper's puppies that played in the back garden and you have a good idea what its appearance was."

Once there was a more unusual visitor, as Mrs Forster told Aunt Laura. "We went through a brief excitement the other day - we saw an odd creature rushing about in a field, it dashed through a hedge and I said as we all did that it was the Franklin's mule - later on hunters and hounds came but still it never occurred to us it was a deer..." Deer were rarely seen in the neighbourhood and one local boy thought the animal was "a queer calf." The unfortunate creature was finally cornered and taken away in a cage "for future use" as it was the custom for those gentlemen who indulged in stag-hunting to transport their quarry by train to the location of their choice.

As the years passed the garden gradually took shape under Mrs Forster's care, each season revealing its own special beauty. Their mutual passion for gardening was one of the bonds that held the family together. Laura Forster and Aunt Monie were particularly keen gardeners, but Maimie also shared their interest, though more moderately. As for Morgan, he had demonstrated a love of flowers from an early age. Aunt Monie, always intensely interested in his development, had realised that he derived pleasure not so much from the overall effect of a garden, as adults did, but from contact with individual flowers. When they were discussing the move to Rooks Nest, Aunt Monie had told Mrs Forster that she was sure Morgan would make her have both flowers and friends, adding, "I never saw a child who more appreciated both than he does..."

When Morgan was very small Aunt Monie sent him a dozen hyacinth bulbs which, she said, would "all blow and grow in glasses in water...but you could if you liked put them in earth in pots." Growing indoor hyacinths became a tradition in the family and every year the Forsters would compare notes with Aunt Monie about the success of their bulbs. Once Mrs Forster had regretfully to report that hers were "rather meagre, one failed altogether." No doubt Morgan took pleasure in watching the progress of his hyacinths; first the brittle white roots reaching untidily into the water, then leaves gradually becoming taller until they were pushed apart by thick, pale green buds which slowly opened to reveal pink, blue or white blooms. Their scent was of course an added attraction, wafting through the house.

19. Hyacinths

On warm, sunny days outdoor activities beckoned. Mrs Forster's friendship with the Jowitts and Postons had revived her interest in tennis and she turned the front lawn into a lawn tennis court, in spite of the fact that its decided slope down into the dell-'ole gave an advantage to players on the house side. Morgan did not share her enthusiasm - he was poor at games - but he did accompany his mother to tennis parties at Highfield and the Rectory. In return the Postons and Jowitts came frequently to Rooks Nest spending happy summer afternoons in the garden, playing games or idling in hammocks.

51

DIVERSIONS

Summer always brought visitors from the Whichelo family. Mrs Forster's aunt, Kate Graham, came regularly. She was not very well off and was often depressed because of this. Mrs Forster, who was fond of her, sometimes helped with gifts of money, for which her aunt was pathetically grateful.

"I do not know how to thank you for your magnificent present. It's the only...money I have," she wrote once. Aunt Kate was useful to Mrs Forster, as she was willing to look after Rooks Nest when her niece went away. On one such occasion, when Aunt Kate decided to undertake some of the domestic chores, she and the maid Phoebe cleaned every window in the house. They were horrified, two days later, to find the landing window covered with what looked like whitewash. "The birds if you please," wrote Aunt Kate, "I almost walk on them..." For Rooks Nest was home to doves, sparrows, starlings and many other birds which had become quite tame through lack of persecution.

In spite of the family and their new friends, the Forsters continued to live very secluded lives. Thanks to the Jowitts, Mrs Forster did take some interest in village life. She was prevailed upon to support local charities, such as the fund to provide an altar frontal and pulpit cloth for the parish church. Her name featured in the list of subscribers, although her contribution of two shillings could not compare with Mrs Jowitt's magnificent donation of £1. The practice of publishing detailed subscribers' lists must have been a subtle way of increasing funds since, in those class-conscious days, no-one would want to be seen giving less than others of the same status.

Life at Rooks Nest settled into a peaceful routine. Every morning after breakfast Morgan had lessons, at first from his mother, and later from a Miss Munt, who taught him the piano and the basics of writing and arithmetic. In the afternoons there were sometimes more lessons, after which he often played with one of the maids or amused himself in the garden. After tea his mother usually played dominoes or a card game with him before he was washed and got ready for bed. Lastly he said his prayers while his mother listened; she sometimes used this duty as a convenient ending to a letter, writing as if in haste, "the boy is waiting to say his prayers so I must fly."

The unhurried pace of life gave Mrs Forster and Morgan time to enjoy the simple pleasures of each season and to find amusement in small, unexpected incidents. The household

DIVERSIONS included a dog and a cat, who were usually referred to by Morgan as "Puppy" and "Kitty." One evening Puppy suddenly started to scramble up Mrs Forster's bedroom chimney, leaving only his hind legs showing, an escapade that sent both mother and son "into fits" as she later told Maimie. Morgan also kept the family up-to-date with news of the Rooks Nest pets. He wrote to his grandmother: "I have had your letter. Puppy's malady is better," adding as an afterthought, "That is a rhyme."

Morgan had learnt to read when he was four: "From that moment I never looked back. Printed words spread around me. No one taught me to read and no one managed to teach me to write."

The latter comment was directed at his handwriting, often subject to criticism by his mother. He was fortunate in that Maimie and Aunt Monie sometimes sent him parcels of books and his mother also shared his enthusiasm for them. Even at this early age Morgan's critical faculties were well-developed. As soon as he was old enough to understand it, his mother tried to make him read *The Story of Our Father's Love* which had been his own father's christening present, but Morgan refused to persevere with it on the grounds that it was insipid. On winter afternoons he would sit reading in front of the drawing room fire, with its ornate Victorian surround until, as the light faded, one of the maids brought a lamp and drew the curtains across the French windows. Sometimes his mother sat with him, busy with crochet work, but more often than not occupied with her correspondence. She had a facility with words which resulted in sharply-observed and amusing letters. This was just as well, since Aunt Monie had insisted that, if Morgan was to be taken away from her to live in the wilds of the country, she must be informed daily of his progress. Aware that Aunt Monie's age and health - she was confined to a wheelchair - made it impossible for her to come to Stevenage, Mrs Forster did her best to comply with the old lady's wishes, but she was often hard put to it to think of something fresh to say. She tried explaining that there was really nothing new to report, but this elicited the sharp reply: "If you please I think I

54

should like to live at Rooks Nest where you tell me nothing ever happens..."

Aunt Monie's letters to Morgan sometimes contained more than the usual family gossip. One of the most interesting described her childhood memory of seeing King George III open Parliament in the year 1804, when she was seven years old, but Morgan was too young to appreciate its historical interest at the time. He was more concerned with her injunction to him: "I think it is time for you to write me another letter. Do you write every day."

As if it were not enough to have one side of the family so energetically engaged in correspondence, Morgan's grandmother, Mrs Whichelo, also had a ready pen and a sense of humour. The effect upon Morgan of so much letter-writing was two-fold. Firstly, it kept Aunt Monie, Gran, Maimie and all his other relatives constantly in his mind. It was clear that they were much more important to his mother than the people among whom she lived, with the result that she never allowed herself to put down roots in Stevenage, but always thought of London as the centre of her existence. This must have been disturbing to Morgan, for whom Rooks Nest was home and security. To hear his mother speak disparagingly of the Franklins or other local people made him unhappy as loyalty to his mother vied with his affection for neighbours and friends.

The second consequence of the literary activity of his mother and aunts may have been to encourage Morgan to write himself. When he was very small, Mrs Forster had composed riddles and rhymes for him and she was pleased when he began to follow her example. He began by making up stories with intriguing titles such as *Screams and Scuffles in the Wardrobe* which was probably sparked off by his games of hide-and-seek in the large built-in cupboard in his nursery. The Rooks Nest cats may have inspired *The Adventures of Pussy Senior* but the origins of *The Earring in the Keyhole* and *Dancing Bell* are more obscure. *Chattering Hassocks* no doubt resulted from Morgan's attendance at the Parish Church. This story so impressed Mrs Forster that she recounted it in a letter to Aunt Monie, who seized on it with enthusiasm, but as usual wanted more. "Why didn't you finish baby's story about the talking hassocks?" she asked. "It's much better than *Alice in Wonderland*. I long for the time when he will be able to write them." Apparently Aunt Monie recognised the future novelist even at this early stage in his career.

As often happens with solitary children, once Morgan had acquired the habit of making up stories, he began to include imaginary events in his conversation. Mrs Forster was horrified at this, writing in some agitation to Aunt Monie for advice on what she considered to be a serious matter of telling lies. Aunt Monie replied in equally anxious vein:

> "I have not an idea what I should do if I had a child who indulged in that stile [sic] of talk, but I do think it ought to be stopped somehow...when in one of his affectionate moods, if you were to talk to him as if he were about 20, and show him the evil consequences of saying what is not true for one thing and what will make mothers who have good children afraid of letting them play with a boy who says such shocking and untrue things...if you could convince that precocious little head of his that it really grieved you, he would reform..."

Lacking brothers and sisters, Morgan was subjected to the full intensity of his family's devotion, but so much loving concern was not easy to live with. Aunt Monie's nickname "The Important One" was certainly apt, but it was a heavy burden to place upon a child, implying that the happiness of his mother and aunt depended entirely upon him: "They centred around me...Too much affection in a world that contains too little is ironical..."

A further example of Aunt Monie's lessons in virtuous living occurred when Morgan went to stay with her at Clapham. "I gave Morgan a bottle of spray scent and advised him whenever he felt naughty to put some on his hands and head and he would infallibly become good and he finds it very efficacious," she once wrote. Deliberate bad behaviour was not really in keeping with Morgan's character, apart from occasional fits of screaming rage, when he flung toys or cushions across the room as a result of boredom or frustration. For the most part he was affectionate and anxious to be thought well of. Aunt Monie herself commended him for his kindness.

Although writing of various kinds occupied Mrs Forster and Morgan a great deal, they also enjoyed more frivolous pastimes. On winter evenings they played dominoes or bezique together, under the gaze of a row of toy animals and dolls. One of these, Sailor Dollar, was Morgan's favourite for a long time, inspiring Mrs Forster to write a soliloquy based on Morgan's conversations with him. Unfortunately, Sailor Dollar was badly treated by his owner, who later bitterly regretted poking his eye out and throwing him over the bannisters. Naturally, all this was recounted to Aunt Monie, who immediately bought a new doll and sent it off to Rooks Nest. Morgan was thrilled to receive the newcomer, whom he named Sailor Duncan, but he did not lose his affection for his old friend.

From time to time Morgan would turn eagerly to a new hobby - model-making, paperfolding, scrapbooks - but as he really had little aptitude for handicrafts, his enthusiasm quickly waned. Stamp-collecting was one activity which did continue, after his mother gave him a stamp album for his ninth Christmas. Thereafter, he and Maimie, who shared the same interest, exchanged stamps for many years.

Anniversaries, Christmas and birthdays were celebrated with due ceremony. Morgan was fairly deluged with presents, and was brought up to write "thank-you" letters as soon as he could control pencil or pen. His earliest were carefully copied, and unmarred by crossings-out, usually ending with the words, "I am your dear Morgan." When he first attempted a more adult version, he spoiled the effect by a spelling mistake; "I remian your dear Morgan."

From a very early age Morgan, who knew the importance of giving, as well as receiving, carefully saved and planned for such occasions. Shortly before his mother's twenty-ninth birthday, when he was five years old, he and the maid Lina went with Mrs Forster in the pony trap to Stevenage High Street. While Mrs Forster went off to pay bills, Morgan and Lina did some shopping on their own account, and when his mother came back, Morgan handed her a wrapped object, saying, "Take care Mamma, it's glass, it costs 6d and it's a secret for your birthday." Mrs Forster pretended that she could not possibly wait to see what it was, and Morgan exhorted her to be patient.

When at last the great day came, Mrs Forster had something to write to Aunt Monie about. "This morning he flew out of bed, dived underneath bed and picked out a cigar box. I struggled with the lid and unpacked a pink glass vase, which didn't surprise me any more than it will you..." Aunt Monie's own gift was hardly more exciting, being a copy of *Hymns Ancient and Modern*. In further recognition of the occasion, Morgan told his mother that he would allow her to win at dominoes, by breaking the rules if need be, after which they had a celebration tea of Vienna bread and plum jam. At times like this Morgan was so happy with his mother that he could imagine no better life, and told her that he intended to marry her when he grew up.

Next year, when his mother's thirtieth birthday approached, Morgan did not do his own shopping, but commissioned Emma to buy the present, giving her $10\frac{1}{2}$d to get it with... "a vase of course - it is his one idea of a birthday present", sighed Mrs Forster. After the gift had been presented, and received with suitable expressions of delight, Morgan suddenly realised that he had spent all his money. "It was most ridiculous," said Mrs Forster. "He laid in a heap on the floor like a beggar, saying 'I never did feel so poor before and don't you think it would almost be better if you paid...'"

At Christmas even Mrs Forster's splendid isolation was eroded a little. A number of people in the village invited Morgan to their children's parties and there were also local concerts and other entertainment. Eight year old Morgan wrote happily to Maimie: "I have been to a party on Friday and am going to another on Thursday." The following year he went with his mother to an evening of drama performed by boys at the Grange School, in the High Street. Morgan enjoyed the evening, being much taken with the costumes, and intrigued by the fact that a boy he knew actually had to eat a jam tart on stage.

Morgan became very excited as Christmas approached, delighting in all the traditional activities of choosing presents, making decorations, cooking cakes and puddings. It was a matter of some importance to him that each member of the household should be given an appropriate gift. One year he noted with satisfaction that the maids, Hide and Mary, were to be given a muff each, while his great friend, Ansell, the garden boy, was to receive a silver chain. He had already decided to give his mother a copy of *Scenes from Clerical Life* and meanwhile he was busily employed, with Hide's help, in making a Christmas banner.

Mrs Forster told Maimie, in a burst of exasperation, "I shall be glad when Christmas is over as I have about 20 presents to buy and don't know what I want exactly and I am always afraid I shall forget somebody. I wish I could dare to abstain from sending Christmas cards." Nor did the snow and frost which fascinate the young hold many charms for Mrs Forster. She woke one Christmas morning to find that all the drinking water had frozen in its containers, and there was no water to cook the Christmas dinner. With some ingenuity she remembered the hot-water bottles and persuaded the maids to re-use the water for cooking. Mrs Forster's thoughts dwelt unkindly on the wickedness of Colonel Wilkinson in denying his tenant her own well, but

21. Snowdrops

Morgan considered that Christmas Day had started most amusingly. The difficulties caused by the freezing weather quite passed him by as he undid his presents in the warmth of a log fire, sheltered from the outside world by the protective walls of Rooks Nest.

4

THE COUNTRYSIDE

An excursion from Rooks Nest into "the village," as Stevenage was then known, was often beset with difficulties as, not being carriage folk, the Forsters relied upon their pony and trap for transport. The pony, a recalcitrant animal, would go no further than it deemed necessary, as Morgan never forgot: "...we did not visit widely, for the pony backed when he thought we were going too far, and ran the trap into a hedge." But since the road from Rooks Nest to Stevenage was downhill, the pony could usually be persuaded to complete the journey, however erratically.

Once they reached the sharp bend in Weston Road, where the Parish Church of St. Nicholas stood with its attendant cottages on one side and the old Bury on the other, there was a choice of routes to the High Street. To the left, the road continued on through farmland, passing Mill Field with its now derelict windmill, and a group of 18th century almshouses still known as the Pesthouses. A little further on there were more cottages as the Weston and Walkern roads merged and finally entered the High Street near the Two Diamonds public house. This was not the road favoured by Mrs Forster, as it led through the dwellings of the poor, and was therefore unattractive. Much pleasanter was the route through Rectory Lane, passing the Rectory and Woodfield and emerging into the Great North Road by the Marquis of Granby inn, near the site of the former turnpike tollgate. Turning into the main road, the trap then passed a few cottages, some with weatherboarded walls and thatched roofs. Children, chickens and dogs ran about in the dusty road, moving unconcernedly out of the way of the occasional farm cart, pony trap or rider on horseback. This was the era of the railway, when road transport, in the form of stage-coaches, was in decline. Shortly they reached the Bury Mead, at the edge of which stood the National School, built in 1834

STEVENAGE. CHURCH CORNER.

22. Church corner,
c. 1910. Weston Road,
leading to Rooks Nest,
is on the right.

to educate the children of the village and next to it, Alleyne's Grammar School and the Grange School.

Morgan's own description of the High Street, written in 1894, begins:

> "And that reminds me I have never said anything about the village...It consisted of one long straggling street built down the London Road. We entered it at the higher end, where the houses each side receded a great deal. The space between them formed what was politely called the Bowling Green, though it would have been a curious ball that could have rolled over it without stopping. However the grass was nice enough to make the village look pretty, and was useful for the fair or for bonfires."

Two centuries earlier, bowls had indeed been played on the green. Samuel Pepys noted in his diary for 1664 that he played a game or two there while waiting for his wife to join him. He had stayed at the Swan, an important coaching inn facing the Bowling Green, but by the time the Forsters arrived in Stevenage its coaching days were over and it had been converted into the Grange School. It was here that Morgan watched the boys' Christmas play, which he enjoyed so much. Although the Bowling Green had apparently deteriorated since Pepys' day, the inhabitants of nineteenth

23. The Avenue, c. 1910

century Stevenage were very attached to it, as it provided them with a natural gathering place for outdoor events.

There was a third way into the village, the one which Morgan loved, but it was only for people on foot or horseback. This was the Avenue, which ran from the Parish Church through fields, across Bury Mead and into the High Street. It began opposite the church as a footpath, opening out about halfway down into a magnificent avenue of horse-chestnuts and limes. It was beautiful at all seasons: in spring, white and pink chestnut candles scented the air with their unique, spicy perfume; in summer, the overhanging boughs gave welcome green shade; gold, brown and red leaves dropped silently down in autumn, with the added interest of

62

"conkers" for children; and winter's graceful bare branches were soon producing their sticky buds, promising a new beginning. Rooks, resident the whole year, started building new nests in January, and at night the trees were haunted by tawny owls.

The Bowling Green, with its surrounding buildings, quickly became familiar to the Forsters, as they had to cross it on their way to the railway station at the top of Julian's Road. After seeing departing guests safely on to the train, they often walked the mile and a half back to Rooks Nest, even when Morgan was very small. When they themselves travelled by train they usually went second class, but once Aunt Monie insisted on giving them the money to buy first class tickets. She was later informed that "...getting into the rail carriage at Stevenage [Morgan] said solemnly to the three people in it...'We never went first class before - Mama and I never - would you tell me what it's like in here.'"

Accustomed as she was to London stores, Mrs Forster regarded Stevenage as the place where she did her marketing for the essentials of day-to-day living. Her dealings with the High Street traders were businesslike and she did not attempt to look below the surface to the busy, interweaving lives of the local people. The High Street had a good range of small shops, quite adequate to the needs of the Rooks Nest household. All the essential trades were represented, including the builders, Bates and Warren, whose premises were next to the Grange. Mrs Forster had many dealings with them. The difficulty of persuading workmen to carry out her instructions was a recurrent theme in her conversation. When she asked for some loose wood blocks in the hall to be stuck down, a man duly arrived to do the job. Unfortunately, he dropped boiling pitch everywhere. "Dust was awful. Smell was awful and boards are still loose," reported Mrs Forster, adding ominously, "So I am going to [berate] Mr Bates tomorrow if I can catch him."

Mrs Forster was almost certainly unaware that Mr Bates' son, Harry, was an unusually talented sculptor, who was later to become a Royal Academician.

The sweep was another villager on whose services Mrs Forster was obliged to depend. The practice of using children to clean chimneys worried her, and when a small boy was sent up the dining room chimney at Rooks Nest, she went outside and watched anxiously until suddenly she saw "a black claw appearing round the chimney pot and then out he came and was put down the hall chimney and I heard him puffing inside there." She was touched by the child's plight: "I gave him some money for himself poor little boy and he seemed pleased."

Like his mother, Morgan was an acute observer of the surface of village life, but he was distanced from its reality. He could not fail to notice, as Charles Dickens had, twenty years before, that the High Street, with its many old coaching inns, was remarkably broad for most of its length. It also suffered from mud in winter because of inadequate drainage, and dust in summer from the rough road and unpaved footpaths. There were no such refinements as pavements. The Local Board was slowly coming to grips with these matters, but was hampered by its own inexperience and by the reluctance of many citizens to pay realistic rates. The Board's long deliberations made uninspiring reading in the local press and, if she bothered with them at all, Mrs Forster considered these matters quite outside her sphere. She was almost self-sufficient at Rooks Nest, content for the village to sort out its own problems.

At the far end of the High Street, known as South End, the buildings were crowded closely together until they ended abruptly at a large open space where the straw plait market was held. Here the villagers would gather to sell their plait to traders who then sold it on to the hat manufacturers of Luton or St Albans. Next to it stood Holy Trinity Church, built in 1861 and extended in 1881. Its raw newness caught Morgan's attention, but he may not have realised that this building gave him a tenuous link with his father. The architect of the church, a nephew of a former Rector of Stevenage, was A.W. Blomfield, with whom the young Edward Morgan Llewellyn Forster had once studied.

From this point the High Street became London Road and continued south out of the town, passing the cricket field and a number of newly built detached and semi-detached houses with large gardens. Morgan's description of them was unflattering; "These ugly new houses much disfigured the road, and one did not get rid of them more than a mile further." The road then passed the Six Hills which had so fascinated Morgan when he first saw them from the train, and thence on through Knebworth, Welwyn, Hatfield and Barnet, into London.

Morgan's view of the village was largely restricted to the High Street. He was never allowed to explore the streets

24. Stevenage High Street and Bowling Green, c. 1900

behind it, although he was dimly aware that "the poor" lived there, in the tiny insanitary dwellings of Back Lane and in the cottages around Letchmore Green. The inhabitants of this district were the people whom the Rector exhorted to

65

send their children to school, even going so far as to introduce a cheaper rate for regular attenders. Penny dinners were another inducement to poor children, who marched down from the school to Miss Cannon's Coffee Tavern for their meal. Sunday School gave the opportunity for joining a lending library and for taking part in the annual treat when tea, games and prizes were provided.

Most of these activities were of no great interest to his mother, and thus Morgan was unaware of them. Poverty and the ugliness which so often attends it, were offensive to Mrs Forster, a characteristic she inherited from her own mother and which Morgan to some extent also shared. This did not imply a lack of compassion, but Gran (Mrs Whichelo), at least, recognised the trait as a fault which was not easily cured. She described to her daughter, Mrs Forster, her revulsion at the tribulations of a family she knew: "How unfortunately ailing Trottie's children are and what very extraordinary ailments they have. Poor little Dolly, I used to be so fond of her! but hearing that she is so plain and poverty-stricken I really don't care for her - it is very wicked of me I know. I'm sorry for myself and feel how wrong it is - but it does not prevent me still not caring for the poor little thing!!"

Although many Stevenage people led very simple lives, they were not allowed - or perhaps did not wish - to feel sorry for themselves. The sufferings of others, particularly those unfortunate enough to live in cities, were brought home to them by such means as the curate's talk with lantern-slides entitled *How the Poor Live*. He told them that "there existed a state of misery, desolation and degradation in London and other large towns such as the people in our country towns and villages would hardly credit." The people of Stevenage responded to the needs of London's poor in various ways. Girls in the Sunday School regularly gathered wild flowers and sent them to a children's hospital where they were gratefully received. Holidays for London children were arranged and it was reported that the cottagers of Stevenage were always pleased to receive these guests - the

66

extra money they were given for their keep was very welcome.

If the tribulations of the poor were remote from Morgan, so also were their pleasures. One of these was the annual Fair, held on September 22nd and 23rd on the Bowling Green and along the High Street. For two nights, local people were swept up into the noise and exuberance of roundabouts and swinging boats, coconut shies and shooting ranges. They bought sweets, toffee apples and rock, had their fortunes told, drank too much and ended up fighting. There was usually an outburst of complaint afterwards, but the following year the fair, granted by Royal Charter in 1281, would be back again. Safely tucked up in bed in his nursery at Rooks Nest, Morgan missed the excitement - and the coarseness. His world was not that of the village people, nor even of the gentry who endeavoured to do them good. He was an onlooker of village life, never truly a part of it.

25. Stevenage Fair.

As he grew from infancy to boyhood Morgan felt the urge to explore further afield in the countryside beyond his immediate surroundings. Unable to forget that her son had been a delicate baby, Mrs Forster was not entirely happy about his developing spirit of adventure. Perversely, much as she had been irritated at the way he clung to her when he was little, she now resented his independence. Torn between the desire to keep him under her eye and her oft-expressed wish that he be less of a cry-baby, she compromised by allowing him to go out provided that he was with a suitable companion. Those maids and garden boys who were deemed trustworthy were now deputed to accompany Morgan on walks and pony rides through the fields, woods and lanes around his home. To Morgan, this was freedom; his great joy

67

was to be out exploring the countryside surrounding Rooks
Nest, secure in the knowledge that the familiar comforts of
home would be waiting when he returned.

Morgan's territory was limited by the length of time he
was permitted to be out, and by the distance he could cover
on foot or on his pony. From Rooks Nest it was natural to
strike north to Chesfield thence into the region between the
villages of Weston and Graveley and it was this country
which Morgan came to think of as his own. An equally
attractive landscape lay in the opposite direction, on the
south side of Weston Road, but apart from his visits to
Highfield, Morgan rarely chose this route, but kept to his
favourite haunts.

Chesfield had once been a flourishing community, with
its own church of St. Etheldreda, but by the mid-fifteenth
century the village had so shrunk that it was merely an
appendage of Graveley and the church was allowed to decay.
By the time Morgan knew it, all that remained was the Park,
one or two cottages and the Manor Farm. Almost in the
farmyard, and overrun by nettles, cow-parsley and ivy, stood
the ruined church, deserted by the human race, but home to
barn-owls.

Today the seclusion and tranquillity of Chesfield have so
far been allowed to remain undisturbed, and the place has a
remarkable feeling of antiquity. It can seem to come alive
with the spirits of peasants and craftsmen from other
centuries, while the farm workers and their animals at
Manor Farm might almost be ghosts from the past. It is easy
to think oneself back in time and to visualise the mediaeval
village clustered round the little church, sheltered from the
elements by the encircling woods. For Morgan the presence
of the much-disliked Wilkinsons cast a shadow over the
Park so that he was always glad to move on, following the
narrow, twisty lane, until he came to the chalkpit, overhung
with beech trees, on a ridge of high ground looking out
across open fields to Graveley.

The chalkiness of the soil around Chesfield made
footpaths across the ploughed fields shine out like beams of
moonlight. The chalk also nourished a wide variety of wild

68

26. Chesfield Chalk pit,
now overgrown with trees

flowers: cowslips, yellow rock-roses, wild orchid, periwinkles
and the more common species such as celandines, primroses
and bluebells. Morgan delighted in searching out and
identifying wild flowers, deriving even more pleasure from
them than from the garden at home. For a while he became
fascinated by the art of pressing flowers, sending his family
home-made flower cards for birthdays and special occasions;
but as he grew older, he preferred to leave the wild plants
undisturbed.

69

27. Bramble

His friend Emma, the good-natured, long-suffering housemaid, often went with him on his country walks. He remembered her always as "such a suitable companion" but, to his lasting shame, when they were out picking primroses one day, he hit her. Her usual humility deserted her and she hit him back. Emma was not much more than a child herself, reacting to severe provocation, but Mrs Forster felt that she had no alternative but to dismiss her. Morgan was sorry and deeply regretted her loss.

The wild flowers also provided food and breeding sites for butterflies. For a time Morgan, like many another boy of his generation, took up the pastime of butterfly collecting, chasing after the fragile creatures with a net, suffocating them in a killing bottle and adding them to his collection. But he was so thrilled one March to find a peacock butterfly so early in the year, that he allowed it to live on one of his pink hyacinths. Then he began collecting caterpillars, so that he could watch their various stages of development, until the life cycle was complete and he had the excitement of seeing a brilliant new butterfly emerge. Mrs Forster herself took a keen interest in this new hobby, encouraging the garden boys to search for caterpillars for Morgan. The first time she watched one spin itself into a cocoon she was quite excited.

On a summer's day, Morgan would loll on the sunny bank at Chesfield, conscious of the scent of clover and wild briar, the hum of bees and the songs of larks, dreaming away his time until his allotted companion became bored, and perhaps suggested a race. Then they would rush off down the hill towards Graveley, a small village bisected by the same Great North Road which ran through Stevenage. It had a

70

church and rectory, several farms, a little school and two inns on the main road. It was not particularly pretty, except as seen from the Chesfield ridge, whence it was beautiful, as the smoke from cottage chimneys, mingling with the distant haze, softened the outlines of buildings, diffusing the sun's power into separate beams of gold. This was one of Morgan's favourite places, and one of Mrs Forster's too. Soon after she had settled in at Rooks Nest, she took her mother to Graveley church. Mrs Whichelo was delighted with "the expanse of air and fields" and the peacefulness of the scene. This was disturbed, as Mrs Forster recalled wryly, when they reached the church. "Mr Pardoe, the clergyman flew out upon us and begged us to come in to tea. We refused and afterwards bitterly repented as it poured in torrents and we had a mile and a half to walk. The church just suited my mother's singular requirements. It was quite dark and hardly anyone in our half of the church, the gentry sit behind a screen in the chancel and the poorer brethren in the body of the church..."

From Graveley, other footpaths led over open fields, joining a network of tracks to Friends Green, Tilekiln Woods, Botany Bay and Weston. On a good day, when the pony was agreeable, Morgan might explore some of these, as far as the village of Weston, which was the outer limit of his territory. Exploring the unknown was sometimes a little frightening, and one such adventure remained in Morgan's memory, to be recalled over sixty years later: "I depended a good deal for company upon the garden boys. With one of them, William (Mr Taylor), I am still in touch and he remembers, as I do, how he led me on the pony into the wilds of Botany Bay."

When the footpaths were too muddy, Morgan could keep to the lane that wound its way past Rooks Nest and on to Weston, by woods and meadows and the occasional cottage. Apart from farm labourers tending their sheep and cattle, clearing ditches, trimming hedges, ploughing or sowing the fields, he was unlikely to meet anyone else unless perhaps one of the neighbouring clergy was parish visiting, or a squire and his lady driving out in their carriage. But

71

THE COUNTRYSIDE

appearances could be deceptive: the peace of the countryside, with its apparently immemorial rhythms of seed-time and harvest, hid the actuality of a rural crisis. Many farmers were going bankrupt or selling up, leaving their former workers with no alternative employment. Times were hard for many country people.

At about the same time that Morgan's horizons began to expand, so too did Mrs Forster's limited social life. Encouraged by Mrs Jowitt and Mrs Poston, she became acquainted with a few people in the villages around Stevenage, including the Pryors of Weston Park. Marlborough Pryor, farmer and landowner was a Justice of the Peace and a leading figure in local affairs. The village was accustomed to look to him for guidance and he gave it freely. The 1880's were years of increasing political awareness among the ordinary people of England, and there was pressure for electoral reform. In an address he gave in 1884 Mr Pryor "...explained the new bill for voting in parliament and suggested what to do with our votes when we had got them..." He also stressed the advantages of education and, referring to the lack of jobs in the district, pointed out the need to look elsewhere for work. Agriculture was in decline and the problem of unemployment in rural areas was a very serious one at this time. Many labourers were out of work, or had been forced to accept reductions in wages. A few even began to take an interest in the trade union movement, a phenomenon that was causing some disquiet to local landowners. The Vicar of Weston, speaking "in a plain and homely manner" to the large number of men and boys assembled at one of his regular mission services, took as his theme "Trust in God" and it was reported in the local press that he "...spoke much of what is uppermost in people's thoughts, viz how they can best be prepared to meet the exigencies of the time...the scarcity of labour and the necessary decreases in wages, both pressing so hard upon them in the coming winter. He referred to meetings in London of the so-called unemployed, and pointed out that nothing could be gained by the manifestation of any spirit of lawlessness."

72

28. The pond in Walkern Road, *c.* 1900, only source of drinking water for the poor who lived nearby.

Although local farmers and landowners, in tune with the times, took advantage of market forces to employ fewer labourers and reduce wages, it was often these same men, or their wives and daughters, who tried to alleviate distress among the poor. Soup kitchens were set up in most villages during the winter months; Mrs Poyntz-Stewart took some responsibility for this at Graveley, while at Stevenage private charity provided penny dinners for school-children twice a week. For the really destitute, especially the aged poor, the ultimate solution remained the workhouse. Stevenage and most of the neighbouring villages were part of the Hitchin Union of Parishes, sharing the use and upkeep of the workhouse at Hitchin. This meant that many elderly Stevenage people spent their last days away from the village where they had lived all their lives, although after death their bodies were usually brought home for burial at the Parish Church. The Board of Guardians at the workhouse were well-intentioned and they carried out their duties conscientiously. Their reports and their advertisements for tenders to supply bread and clothing for the inmates or for "outdoor relief" were all in accordance with the

73

requirements of the law. Nevertheless, Hitchin Workhouse
was not an attractive place. An article in the *Stevenage Local
Magazine*, exhorting people to save for their old age,
suggested that those who did not see the need for this should
visit the old people's wards of a workhouse.

Some men preferred to avoid the workhouse, or even the
less humiliating "outdoor relief" (that is, the provision of
basic rations to keep people alive in their own homes) by
taking to the open road, tramping from village to village in
search of work, sometimes reduced to begging. Morgan was
used to tramps, as they often called at Rooks Nest, where the
inner and outer doors of the back porch were useful for
keeping them at bay. Next door at Rooks Nest Farm tramps
could anticipate a kinder reception, as Mrs Franklin made it
a principle never to deny them food or drink.

At harvest time the ancient practice of gleaning corn left
behind after a field had been cut was important to the
villagers, who relied upon it to help feed their livestock.
Because people depended so much upon the corn they
collected in this way, many villages set time limits for
gleaning, to ensure that the younger and more able-bodied
did not rush to the fields and take all the corn before the aged
or infirm could get there. At Stevenage the gleaners' bell was
rung at 7 am and 7 pm and gleaning was allowed only
between those times. Previously, one of the bells at the
Parish Church had been rung for this purpose, but from 1883
the Holy Trinity bell in the High Street was used, as it was
nearer to the centre of population.

Gleaners must have been a familiar sight to Morgan as he
wandered along the footpaths and across stubble fields in late
summer. They moved slowly forward, bending low to fill
their sacks, occasionally stopping to stretch their limbs or
chat with a neighbour. They were mostly women with small
children scampering around them, but there were some old
men, and even a few younger ones in hard times. To
Morgan they made a pleasant rural picture, illustrating one
of the scenes of the country calendar. Harvest time brought
also the sight of men and boys with guns, encircling the last
tiny refuge of standing corn left uncut in the centre of a field,

74

where rabbits had thought themselves safe from the reapers. As this cover too was destroyed, rabbits fled in all directions and many were killed among great shouting and hubbub. Morgan accepted these scenes as part of life, but he did not relish them.

During the winter months he was kept indoors for much of the time, and was little aware of the hunting and shooting that went on annually around Rooks Nest. Hounds met at Chesfield Park, attracting people of all classes, the gentry and farmers on horseback and other enthusiastic followers on foot. Many a fox lay hidden in the wooded countryside, which was ideal for game. Shooting parties were held regularly in the frosty fields and when the sportsmen had gone home to convivial gatherings, it was the turn of poachers. Sport of any kind bored Morgan and he was content to leave his fields and woods until spring, when he could again explore in peace.

The cruelties and hardships of country life did not penetrate deeply into Morgan's consciousness, as he searched for wild flowers, stopped to gaze, or rushed madly along in some game with his companion. Old women gathering firewood, young women gleaning, ragged men tramping the lanes and labourers whose working day stretched from dawn to dusk were for him symbols of the countryside, defining the seasons, at one with the landscape. Just as he thought of Rooks Nest as a living entity, affording him protection and security, so he felt the land around had a spirit of its own, which dwelt in men, animals, plants and earth alike.

29. Horse Chestnut candle

Mrs Forster was pleased that her son was so well and happy, but she could not realise that he was developing an attachment to the place which was as strong as many another child's affection for a human being. To her, Rooks Nest was somewhere to live. For him, it was "the abiding city."

5
1887

For as long as Morgan could remember, his Great Aunt Monie had dominated family life. Although unmarried and childless, she had assumed a matriarchal role and was regarded with considerable respect by her nephews and nieces. Her wealth, together with her circle of friends which included Lord Macaulay, Florence Nightingale, William Wilberforce and other leading figures of the Victorian age, added to her prestige. Inevitably she was deferred to, and she grew accustomed to having her own way, but she was also kind, generous and very wise, as Morgan was quick to recognise. Mrs Forster had every reason to be grateful to Aunt Monie, since she had gone to live with her as "a shy little girl of 12." Her own family, the Whichelos, were not well-off and when, after a chance meeting, the philanthropic Miss Thornton offered to educate her for the career of governess, her widowed mother was delighted. The arrangement was successful, and in due course the young Lily Whichelo met Edward Morgan Llewellyn Forster, Aunt Monie's favourite surviving nephew, and became engaged to him at the age of 23. Some members of the Thornton family had reservations about the engagement, but Aunt Monie herself was very happy.

When, following the death of her husband, the young Mrs Forster moved to Stevenage, she was careful not to damage the ties of affection between herself and Aunt Monie. She was well aware of the old lady's love for Morgan and a constant stream of correspondence flowed between Rooks Nest and Clapham. Yet each year it became harder to maintain a balance between independence and duty, as Aunt Monie asked for more, and longer, visits. As for Morgan, his affectionate nature made him sympathetic to the problems of old age and he was genuinely appreciative of Aunt Monie's love and generosity towards him, but he was not wholly at ease in her company, finding her devotion difficult to live up to. The dark house at Clapham depressed him and he longed to be back at Rooks Nest, as did his mother, who had to resign herself annually to abandoning her garden for weeks at a time. "I do wish we were at home to enjoy the nice spring, it does seem such a pity after being at home during the winter to leave it, just as it is nicer, but we have to do it every year," she told Aunt Laura.

In 1887 Aunt Monie was ninety and in failing health. She could not get about without her wheelchair and relied upon a nurse to look after her. Even her favourite pastime of letter-writing began to be a burden, as she explained to Morgan on his eighth birthday, when she sent him the generous gift of a magic lantern. "This is a dull note, but the fog has got into everything I think - I am so very old that I can hardly expect to be alive another year to wish you a happy new year, that we cannot tell, but I do know what a joy and pleasure you are now to everyone about you."

Such a letter could not fail to move Mrs Forster, so she took Morgan to stay at Clapham several times that year. Their visits were made less pleasant than they might have been by the presence of Henrietta Synnot, Aunt Monie's niece and companion who was also Morgan's Godmother. For some reason she had never much liked Mrs Forster, but over the years dislike had turned almost to hatred, so that she now refused even to be in the same room with her. "H. has no lights and shades in her friendships, it is all *fortissimo* and *pianissimo*," wrote Mrs Forster in exasperation. Henrietta's method of expressing dislike usually took the peculiar form of the gift of a religious text, such as a prayer book. A Bible was a mark of supreme displeasure and Mrs Forster could interpret only too clearly the symbolism of her present to Morgan during their first visit in 1887, "Bye the bye she (H.) sent for Morgan just before she left and gave him a Bible! I suppose she thought that with such a mother it was her duty to provide him with religious sustenance..."

Shortly after this episode Mrs Forster's patience deserted her and she gave vent to long-restrained annoyance by writing a "strong" letter to Henrietta, telling her exactly what

1887 she thought of her behaviour. This had the desired effect in that Henrietta was at last subdued, but Aunt Monie was saddened by the open admission of animosity. Morgan was aware of the "war with H." as his mother described it, but it did not affect him greatly, beyond giving him one more reason for disliking Aunt Monie's house.

Life at Clapham was not very enjoyable for Morgan. When he was small he had delighted in playing with the toys which Aunt Monie kept for the amusement of young relatives. There was a clockwork French lady who, once wound up careered madly round the room, crashing into the legs of both furniture and Mrs Forster. "My dear, you never give her room," Aunt Monie would say defensively. An assortment of toy animals, including a white furry rabbit which could be made to hop, lost their attraction for Morgan as he grew older. It was a relief to escape from Aunt Monie's house with his grandmother, Mrs Whichelo, who came to breakfast one morning and took him to visit the Natural History Museum and the Kensington Museum. "I should guess [she] is dead today, judging by what I hear of their goings on," wrote Mrs Forster next day. Morgan told his mother that he liked excursions of this kind, to see "something really interesting" far better than those which were merely entertaining. In a rather condescending manner he described an idol he had seen, adding, when she showed some confusion over its name, "You are making a little mistake." He went on to explain further. "He told me the names, which I had never heard of, which is the case with many other things he tells me," said Mrs Forster.

In spite of his preference for intellectual activities, Morgan did not refuse an outing to see the famous American cowboy, "Buffalo Bill." Mrs Forster was a little worried that the show might frighten him, but he said resignedly that he did not expect anything else. Quoting a newspaper advertisement which promised: "To the favoured visitor Buffalo Bill will show an enemy's scalp and the knife he scalped him with," Mrs Forster remarked, "I am thankful to [think] that there is no chance of my being so distinguished." In the event, both mother and son enjoyed the show, in

78

which Red Indians complete with warpaint and feathers noisily attacked a log cabin, only to be beaten back by Buffalo Bill and his cowboys with "much shooting and screaming."

Whilst they were staying at Aunt Monie's Mrs Forster did occasionally have some time to herself. After the exciting Buffalo Bill show she put Morgan to bed before going on to see some *tableaux vivants* in which her friends the Alfords were performing. But it was not easy to get away from Aunt

30. Marianne Thornton as a young woman

Monie, as she explained on refusing Laura's invitation to stay with her in Surrey: "Much as I should like to see you and the flowers I dare not suggest it to Monie as we are rather full of engagements..." An earlier visit to Mrs Whichelo had been kept secret. "We went to my mother for 2 days and I did not tell Monie at the time and don't mean to now as she would feel aggrieved," Mrs Forster told Maimie in a letter from Clapham, in which she signed herself, "Your loving woebegone Lily."

Aunt Monie was becoming increasingly difficult. Not only did she want Morgan with her, but she constantly invited people to see him, showing him off like a prized possession, much to his mother's annoyance: "Monie leads one such a life. She will ask Smith, Jones and Robinson to come and see Morgan - not for any particular day - I could bear that better..."

At length they were able to return to Stevenage, where they found the whole district preparing to celebrate Queen

79

1887 Victoria's Golden Jubilee. Every town and village planned to mark the occasion, with the result that there was a great flurry of fund-raising activity everywhere. Progress reports on the Women's Offering to the Queen appeared weekly in the local press; Stevenage subscribed £14..4..5, Weston £5..5..0 and Walkern £4..2..0. In this latter village, it was noted, all who gave did so cheerfully; only six refused and only one refused "ungraciously."

The one Walkern villager who refused ungraciously had her counterpart in Mrs Forster. Her strong political views amounted almost to republicanism and she objected to the very idea of celebrating the monarch's jubilee, let alone to contributing money towards such an event. It is possible that a number of other people agreed with her, but most were too apathetic, or too cautious, to say so publicly, particularly in a small village where it would not be expedient to offend the "lady collectors." However, the majority were pleased to have an occasion to look forward to, something out of the ordinary which would be talked about to children and grandchildren. Many genuinely respected and admired the Queen, both for her integrity and as a symbol of national life. This view was shared by Aunt Monie who was quite upset to hear of Mrs Forster's attitude. When she discovered that Morgan, under the influence of his mother, had also become a fervent anti-royalist, Aunt Monie wrote him an instructive letter, pointing out Queen Victoria's virtues and the benefits of having a monarchy. But Mrs Forster allowed neither these reproaches, nor the fact that the Jowitts and the Pryors were leading organisers of the local celebrations, to influence her, and she resolutely turned her back on the Jubilee.

The isolated situation of Rooks Nest, coupled with his mother's attitude, combined to insulate Morgan from the excitement of his compatriots. Down in Stevenage village there was heated debate over a proposal to plant trees along the High Street and London Road as far as the Six Hills. A full programme was arranged for the day itself, beginning at 10 a.m. when a procession, headed by a large banner proclaiming "God Save the Queen", moved from the Bowling Green, through the Avenue, to the parish church

80

where the Rector conducted a service of thanksgiving. At one o'clock over 900 adults, seated at tables on the Bowling Green, partook of a meal of beef, new potatoes, pickles, beer and plum pudding. In the afternoon there were sports for both adults and children, after which the day ended with the arrival of the Stevenage Fire Engine "well-manned and well-horsed" and the singing of the national anthem.

Having made their views known, Morgan and his mother took no part in the Stevenage celebrations. Then, unexpectedly, Mrs Forster decided to be in London for the Jubilee procession there, going on to Aunt Monie afterwards. Morgan graciously consented to accompany her and watched the parade with apparent reluctance.

Twelve miles south of Stevenage, the small town of Hatfield flourished in the shadow of Hatfield House, ancestral home of the Cecil family who had been active in English politics since William Cecil, Lord Burghley, became Minister of State to Queen Elizabeth I. In 1887 his descendant, the third Marquess of Salisbury, was Prime Minister to Queen Victoria, in whose honour he gave a garden party at Hatfield House. The guest list included people from most parts of Hertfordshire, Stevenage being represented by Rector and Mrs Jowitt. Many guests, including the Queen herself, travelled by train. The Great Northern Railway Company did not content itself with running special trains; it also built a new waiting room for Queen Victoria at Hatfield station. As well as those fortunate enough to have been invited, many other people gathered in the streets to watch the royal carriage drive past. Once again Morgan found his principles being overruled as, possibly through the intervention of the Jowitts, he was taken to Hatfield and made to stand with other children at a suitable vantage-point along the route. Here the prevailing atmosphere of excited anticipation soon overcame him and, with some other boys, he climbed on to a wall to see better, even cheering and waving his cap when the Queen appeared.

As the summer of 1887 faded it became obvious that Aunt Monie was deteriorating. Mrs Forster took Morgan to stay at Clapham again in September that year, and this was the last time they saw her. Morgan was relieved when they returned to Rooks Nest, but knowing that Aunt Monie was so ill he asked his mother about her repeatedly. At the beginning of November his question was answered with the unexpected words, "She is better," but spoken in such a strange voice that he knew something dreadful had happened. He wept when he finally understood.

Ever since Morgan's birth, Mrs Forster had been aware that Aunt Monie intended to leave him a substantial sum of money, a matter which they had discussed quite openly. "Oh dear," Aunt Monie had written some years earlier, "how I do wish one knew beforehand what children are going to turn out, specially Mr Morgan Forster - as to getting his money when 21 or 25...If he takes it as they call it at 21 no provision is made for his children. If he waits till 25 he is to leave his money for you and his children. I'm afraid this will put it in to his head to marry." Previously she had said it was no use trying to legislate for future generations: "let Morgan make ducks and drakes of his money and take the consequences - "

In her will, Aunt Monie left Morgan £8,000 to be invested and the interest used for his education. He would receive the capital on his twenty-fifth birthday. She also left him the toys he had played with at Clapham; they were now old and dirty, but the Forsters were pleased to have them for sentimental reasons. There was a little unpleasantness with Henrietta over some books which she thought Morgan should not have had, and another small controversy over a paper knife which Aunt Kate Graham requested. Mrs Forster gave in over this, saying sanctimoniously, "tho' I should value it very much it is a far greater pleasure to me to know that Monie wished me to have it than to possess it."

The provisions of Aunt Monie's will did not make a great impression on Morgan at the time. Although Mrs Forster, too, had benefited from it, the £2,000 she received did not change her way of life at Rooks Nest. Indeed, she told Maimie, she felt that the extra money would be a stumbling block to her, as now her own family would expect her to spend it on them. She went on, "...I do feel a good deal annoyed sometimes when I hear and see them all doing and

buying things that I should never dream of. I think perhaps I
am not naturally extravagant and I don't know many others
in my family who take after me." Morgan's strongest
reaction was relief that he would no longer be torn away
from his beloved home to the gloom of Clapham. When he
heard that Aunt Monie's house was to be sold he exclaimed,
"Oh, do you think anyone will be found to take it? Of course,
I liked Aunt Monie in it, but it was such a dreadful house.
We all felt that didn't we...?" Then, thinking of Henrietta
with no friendly home to comfort her, he added, "How she
must envy us." It was not until he was grown-up that
Morgan fully appreciated what Aunt Monie had done for
him. Her legacy made him financially independent as a
young man, at that crucial period before he was established
in his chosen career. He was later to atone for his youthful
indifference by writing *Marianne Thornton, a domestic
biography, 1797-1887,* which was published in 1956. It
concludes with the words: "I have hunted in the tangled
churchyard...for her grave but have failed to find it. She
made a will which was of the greatest importance to me,
though I did not know it at the time...This £8,000 has been
the financial salvation of my life. Thanks to it, I was able to
go to Cambridge - impossible otherwise, for I failed to win
scholarships. After Cambridge I was able to travel for a
couple of years, and travelling inclined me to write...I am   31. Seed heads
thankful...to Marianne Thornton; for she and no-one else
made my career as a writer possible, and her love, in a most
tangible sense, followed me beyond the grave.

6
SCHOOL LOOMING

"Education" was a word frequently on the lips of Morgan's family. From infancy he understood that one day he would go away to school and, in the distant future, to university. Meanwhile, in order to be ready for these experiences it was important for him to work hard at his lessons at home. Not that learning was any hardship to Morgan; his intelligent, inquiring mind coupled with his lonely situation made him eager to acquire knowledge for its own sake. Ironically, this made him more aware of his isolation, since the maids and garden boys who were his chief companions could not understand half the things he wanted to talk about, and there was no one else near his own age with whom he could share facts and ideas.

Mrs Forster, who had been a governess before her marriage, watched Morgan's early progress anxiously. When he was very young she taught him herself, later employing a Miss Munt to teach him arithmetic and English. He also received music lessons and Mrs Forster noted with some asperity: "He gets on well with his music - but with nothing else. Miss Munt is too easy going." Morgan's handwriting was not up to standard either, she told Aunt Monie, adding, "I never can bear things badly done." A little later, his mother decided that Morgan needed firmer handling, and she engaged Mr Hervey, a master at the Grange School, to be his tutor.

Mr Hervey's presence was the cause of some discord in the family. He managed to ingratiate himself with Mrs Forster, who became uncharacteristically friendly and talkative in his company. Her mother, Mrs Whichelo, observed their increasing intimacy with alarm; in her opinion, the tutor was a very uninteresting man. She was relieved when, whether through tact or from conviction, her daughter indicated that she was confiding in him less. "I am pleased that you do not now tell Mr Hervey all your business," she remarked. Morgan was in complete agreement with his grandmother. He judged Mr Hervey to be snobbish and humourless and he particularly disliked the man's condescending attitude towards his friend Ansell. Nor did he ever have cause to change his mind, referring in later life to "my dubious tutor."

Now that he had a tutor, Morgan discovered that life was full of restrictions. He could no longer run out into the meadow just when he felt like it, nor enjoy noisy, hilarious games with the garden boy. Such simple pleasures were frowned upon as childish by Mr Hervey, whose uninspiring lessons Morgan was forced to endure. This hardship was made worse by the knowledge that his mother would have no sympathy with her son. Mrs Forster was flattered by Mr Hervey's attentions, and may even have received a proposal of marriage from him but, to the relief of her family, nothing came of the friendship in the end, although her frequent drives out with him caused some anxious moments.

Education is not merely the means whereby children acquire skills, facts and figures, but a much broader concept encompassing, as Mrs Forster well knew, the whole realm of culture. In this sense, compared with the village children at Stevenage, Morgan was already educated. The journeys by train to London and other places, which he took as a matter of course, were something quite outside their experience. Visits to museums, exhibitions and theatres were enjoyable, but unexceptional, treats to Morgan, whereas many of the village children had never been away from their birthplace. When, very occasionally, a special arrangement was made for them to go further afield, this merited the attention of the local press. In 1886 the Colonial and Indian Exhibition was held in London, and Miss Smith took the sixteen girls who had been most regular attenders at her needlework class to see it. The *Hertfordshire Express* reported: "They started in the morning by the excursion train at 8.51 and proceeded to the exhibition by the Metropolitan Railway...several of the girls had never been further from home than Hitchin." At the same time Mr Pryor of Weston Park "most liberally" treated the Weston choirboys to the exhibition. They were

85

conveyed to Stevenage station in a farm wagon and when they returned in the evening "...the village was quite alive with mothers anxious to see their boys home safe and sound from the metropolis."

In spite of the number of private preparatory schools in Stevenage, Morgan was destined for boarding school on the south coast. He was aware of this, facing the prospect bravely, even with some excitement at the thought of making new friends. He did not anticipate being unhappy and although he loved his life at Rooks Nest, he knew that school was an inevitable part of growing up. Surprisingly, Aunt Monie seems to have been the only one who realised that Morgan was ill-prepared for life at boarding school, as she warned Mrs Forster: "...with school looming in the distance I suppose he must look forward to the time when you will be his refuge from the torments his fellows will bestow upon what they call cheek."

Yet Mrs Forster did not show Morgan much understanding as he grew older. Inevitably, like any other boy, he became rather gawky as he reached the teenage years and his arms and legs seemed to outgrow his body. His mother considered him clumsy and awkward and did not hesitate to tell him so. Loving her as much as ever, Morgan scarcely realised that she was subtly changing. Formerly she had had a tendency to irritability and impatience, but these had been softened by her natural kindness and tempered by prudence. Now that she was accustomed to an independent life she allowed herself to speak sharply or sarcastically as she felt inclined and held herself in awe of no-one, the more so since Aunt Monie's death. This boded ill for her relationship with a number of people with whom it would have been wiser that she kept on good terms. Morgan watched the preparations for his departure with resignation.

His school clothes and books were packed into a large trunk, together with a few prized possessions including his stamp album and butterfly net. Mrs Forster was more concerned with warm underclothes and supplies of cough medicine; Morgan was to be included with the "delicate"

86

boys who were not allowed outdoors in cold weather, nor permitted to take part in strenuous activities.

One autumn day in September 1890, Morgan and his mother set off in the pony trap for Stevenage station. Looking back at the serenity of Rooks Nest, Morgan was overcome by the realisation that the life of the place would carry on without him and he would have no part in it. He knew instinctively that although he would return, it would never be quite the same again. As the pony proceeded in its usual erratic manner, he gazed at the familiar landscape as if seeing it for the first time; the ploughed fields, the parish church, Rectory Lane, the Avenue, the Bowling Green and finally, the station where he would begin his journey to a new life. Once on the train, his melancholy left him as a natural curiosity took over. Above all, he was determined to be a credit to his mother.

When Morgan arrived at Kent House Preparatory School in Eastbourne he was impressed by the kindness of Mr and Mrs Hutchinson, the headmaster and his wife. He wrote to his mother that the boys seemed very nice and he enjoyed the food. "I will tell you what we had for dinner today as an example - roast beef, vegetable marrow, potatoes, plum tart, blackberry tart, jam tart." His main anxiety was for missing collar studs which, he complained, his mother had forgotten to pack. Pleased to know that he was settling in so well, Mrs Forster wrote with unwonted sentimentality "First Letter" across the top of the page.

As the term went on, Morgan discovered that the norms and values of school life were not always the same as those which had obtained at home. He worked diligently at his lessons and was law-abiding to the point of priggishness. Having had no previous experience of school, nor even of brothers and sisters, he did not understand that other boys were not, like him, obsessed with the desire to please their parents, nor that gentleness and innocence were no protection against bullying and ignorance. The school seems to have provided a broad range of extra-mural activities; the boys were often taken up on to the downs, to the sea at Eastbourne, to the swimming baths and on other local

87

excursions. Morgan enjoyed these outings, describing them in detail in his letters home, but as one of the "delicate" boys he was not allowed to join in all the outdoor activities, a restriction which he accepted without complaint, but which did not put him in very good standing with his classmates. Disillusionment came swiftly and he wrote to his mother, "I think I will tell you I am not happy." Once he had admitted this the full force of homesickness came upon him and he bitterly regretted being cut off from all that he loved. He even missed the Rooks Nest cat and dog, although he had never been particularly fond of them when at home; now his letters included admonitions to "take care of kitty." Memories of home flooded back as he waited anxiously for news, consumed with anxiety if his mother's letters were late. "You have neglected me this week. I was afraid you had met with an accident," he wrote to her.

Life was not continuously unhappy. There were brighter moments, such as the occasion of the paper-chase, one of the few sporting activities in which Morgan took part; the Bonfire Night when the whole school gathered for fireworks bought jointly by the boys; the time when soldiers practised manoeuvres on the downs and Morgan watched, enthralled; the entertainment given by a magician; and the kindness of Mr and Mrs Beveridge, parents of one of Morgan's contemporaries. At one stage he was sufficiently happy and engrossed to forget to write his weekly letter home, which omission prompted Mrs Forster to accuse her son of neglecting her. Filled with remorse, he replied immediately, "I will not neglect you again and promise to write twice in the week."

32. School photograph from Kent House, annotated by Morgan

Now his homesickness was made worse by the feeling that it was almost wrong to enjoy himself, as that must mean he was forgetting his mother. In fact, his spells of happiness were brief and any small thing which went wrong served to magnify his longing for home. His loneliness was increased by the fact that many of the boys, as well as being tougher than he was, had brothers at the school. But he "had nothing and no-one to love." Mrs Forster came to see him sometimes and he looked forward eagerly to those days but was

88

philosophical when she failed him, writing with an assurance he probably did not feel "...do not come on Wednesday if you have a headache, as it would spoil your pleasure and mine." Occasionally there were visits from Maimie or one of his aunts and once to his great delight he met an old friend from home as he was taking part in a school walk. He wrote to his mother in great excitement:

"Dear Mamma,

I have rather a lot to tell you. I am going out directly after dinner this afternoon with May Poston...Fortunately Mr Hutchinson was out with us so she went up there and then and asked if I might come to tea..." May Poston had an exceptionally sweet nature, and no doubt she gave Morgan a happy time in her company as she brought him up to date with family news.

Most of Morgan's letters home began with careful descriptions of his state of health, in accordance with his mother's instructions, and ended with enquiries after family and friends. Once he injured his arm quite badly and remembering his mother's opinion of his clumsiness, he wrote ruefully, "You will never guess what your awkward son has done; I have sprained my arm." The injury did not respond well to treatment and Morgan's next letter gave further details, including a startling drawing showing that one of his elbows was almost twice the size of the other. "On Saturday I went to the masseuse...First I had nearly entirely to undress, to take off my coat, waistcoat and shirt, and to unbutton my combinations to slip my arm out, then she rubbed in salad oil...then she looked at it and fetched another lady and they both said it was most singular...I hope you do not feel dull. I feel dull, at least rather, but mine will wear off...I have a snuffly cold, not bad, but it irritates other people. Give my love to Mary and Annie and yourself..."

But Morgan's dullness did not wear off. His thoughts dwelt constantly on going home and he was in a continual state of anxiety lest there should be a muddle over holiday dates or travel arrangements, so that he would somehow be lost, and never reach Rooks Nest. He longed to be with his mother, writing nostalgically after church one Sunday, "We

90

have just had *The Saints of God*, it reminded me of you." However, although she missed her son's company, Mrs Forster had much to occupy her while he was away at school. Her friendship with the Postons deepened and she spent a good deal of time with them and also, to Morgan's disapproval, with Mr Hervey. She wrote to Morgan, "...if fine tomorrow I shall take Mr Hervey for a drive. I do hope the pony will behave...Mind you write to Mr Hervey. You could write a little at a time to make a nice long letter he would like to know all about everything."

At first Mrs Forster seemed not to realise the depth of Morgan's misery and was quite content for him to remain at the school. Then she received a confused letter from Morgan in which he told her of an incident which occurred while he was out walking on the downs. He came unexpectedly upon a man who submitted him to some kind of indecent exposure or sexual assault. To his further confusion, Mrs Forster was horrified and insisted that the headmaster be told and the police notified. She explained to Morgan that he might have to testify in court, and sent her solicitor, Mr Times, to talk to him. The episode had upset and confused Morgan at the time, but he was rather bewildered at the panic it had caused and wrote to reassure his mother,"I did have a shock at first, but not so bad as you seem to expect, I have nearly got over it now."

After a while, it seemed best to allow the matter to drop, and for a time Morgan's life at Kent House resumed its usual pattern. In spite of his determined efforts to make friends he was still finding it difficult to mix with the other boys. Academically he was doing well; his report for Christmas 1892 stated: "Conduct v. good. Has this term obtained a much firmer grasp of his work," but this was little compensation for overwhelming loneliness and homesickness. Perhaps Mrs Forster now read her son's letters with more attention, alert for any hint of danger. Maybe she listened with more sympathy to his descriptions of the petty cruelties he suffered at the hands of his school-fellows. Whatever the reason, in the spring term of 1893 she at last recognised the depth of his unhappiness and removed him from the school.

SCHOOL LOOMING Morgan was immensely relieved at this decision, but his joy at returning to Rooks Nest was dimmed. His experience of preparatory school life had left him lacking in confidence and with little reason to hope that public school would be any better. A cloud of depression hung over him, seeming to dull the beauty of his home surroundings, so that he could no longer feel completely at peace there. In any event he was not free to enjoy it for long, since Mrs Forster had arranged that he should finish the academic year by spending the summer term as a boarder at the Grange School, in Stevenage High Street. The headmaster, the Reverend John Lingen Seager, was a friend of the Jowitts and Mrs Forster felt confident that this was the ideal solution. For his part, Morgan was so glad to be back in a familiar setting that even the prospect of school seemed bearable. He was determined to make the best of his time at the Grange for the short period he would be there, and he wrote cheerfully to his mother on May 10th 1893:

"Dear Mother,
Thank you very much for your letter, caterpillar and sponge-bag. I am getting on very well indeed. I have very quickly got into the ways of the school. I feel I have been there several years...
I am longing to see you dear mother,
Your loving
Morgan."

Confident that Morgan was happily settled at the Grange, Mrs Forster returned to her own affairs. Within a fortnight she had a letter from her son, telling her, "I am threatened with all the school setting on me tomorrow. I rather hope they do, and I don't intend to stand still and be bullied, and perhaps I shall get on better afterwards." His mother no doubt felt a twinge of alarm on reading this, but was perhaps reassured by her son's apparent confidence. A day or two later she received such an anguished letter from him that she went down to the school to find out what was happening. Morgan was incoherent with misery when she arrived, but she could not discover exactly why, except that he had suffered some bullying.

At the age of fourteen, when the torment was actually happening, Morgan was unable to describe it in terms that

92

adults would understand. Not until 1907, when he wrote *The Longest Journey*, was he able to express his anguish. Then, in Chapter 3 of this semi-autobiographical novel, the pain of his schooldays was exposed: "An apple-pie bed is nothing, pinches, kicks, boxed ears, twisted arms, pulled hair, ghosts at night, inky books, befouled photographs, amount to very little by themselves. But let them be united and continuous, and you have a hell that no grown-up can devise."

Mrs Forster was in a dilemma. Her chief confidante in the matter of Morgan's education was Mrs Jowitt, who had helped her arrange the transfer to the Grange. Mrs Jowitt naturally had great faith in the Revd. John Lingen Seager, who, like his father before him, was prominent in local society. It seemed unlikely to Mrs Jowitt that there could be any fault in the running of the school, and so she tended to dismiss Morgan's problems as a temporary setback, soon to be forgotten. On the other hand, his unhappiness was patently obvious, not least to Maimie who happened to be staying at Rooks Nest at the time. Her sympathies were very much with Morgan. To complicate matters further, she and Mrs Jowitt did not get on and poor Mrs Forster could only consult each separately.

33. Dormitory at the Grange School

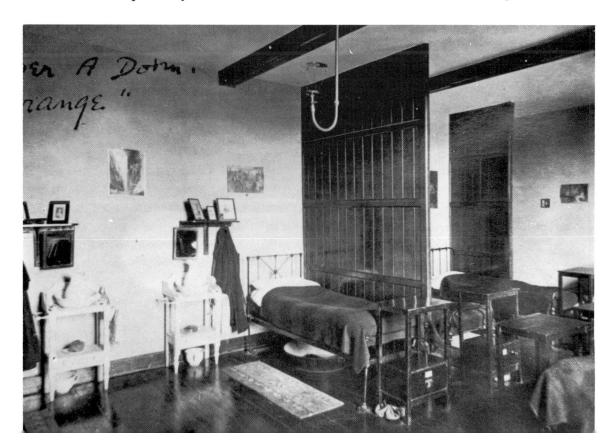

SCHOOL
LOOMING

The weekend of May 27th and 28th 1893 took on a nightmare quality. Mrs Forster had had a rather unsatisfactory conversation with Mrs Jowitt on the previous Friday, after which she decided that she was probably making too much fuss of her son, and would be sensible to take no further action. But she was preoccupied, and could not enjoy Maimie's company. On Monday an hysterical letter arrived from Morgan:

"Dear Mother,
Why have you not come, what are you going to do?...O what is going to happen? I felt I could not say anything when you came. I feel utterly wretched. I would like to come away. Everyone is against me except Squire and Sworder...I have tried to keep from breaking down but I could not help it and all the boys have noticed it. Goodbye from your loving son Morgan."

Mrs Forster acted immediately and by the evening of May 29th Morgan was home at Rooks Nest. His mother was rather embarrassed at having removed him so suddenly and she was anxious not to offend the Seagers, and thereby, the Jowitts. She wrote apologetically to Mr Seager:

"I should be very sorry to cause you any annoyance...when I found [Morgan] in a state of abject terror yesterday afternoon at the thought of passing another night exposed to the chance of boys from other dormitories coming in to annoy him I felt it was time something was done to release him. On Sunday night 4 or 5 boys were going at him at once...Many of the boys used bad language and his refusing to do the same has been another reason for his unpopularity...had it not been for the boys Morgan would have been quite happy, he enjoyed his work with you and speaks warmly of Mrs Seager's kindness."

Mrs Jowitt, who heard the news as she was on the point of leaving for a visit to her family home at Altrincham, wrote a hasty note to Mrs Forster: "I hope very much I did not vex or hurt you in any way by anything I said, or left unsaid, on Friday; I am very sorry if I did - indeed I have learnt to mistrust sorely my own judgement..." Mrs Forster reassured her, explaining the circumstances more fully, whereupon Mrs Jowitt replied: "...it's infinitely better for M. to be idle at home or unsettled in his work than to lower his standards of truthfulness and honour, from that you have saved him..."

94

Unpleasant though the bullying and coarseness had been, both at Kent House and the Grange, they were not the sole cause of Morgan's unhappiness. A contributory factor was his loss of security, as it gradually became clear to him that his mother intended to leave Rooks Nest. After years of deteriorating relationships with her landlords, first Colonel Wilkinson and now the Poyntz-Stewarts, Mrs Forster decided to move elsewhere. She had apparently made up her mind as soon as Morgan went off to Kent House, but did not tell him at first, knowing he would be upset. When she did break the news he was horrified and almost physically ill. He wrote from Kent House, "…what with the moving and other things it makes me feel bad. I was not well yesterday (Sunday) so I had to finish my letter today…"

Once she had told him of her decision, Mrs Forster no longer had to keep her house-hunting a secret from Morgan and she made a point of telling him how she was getting on. As far as she was aware he had become resigned to the idea, provided that they lived in the country. He reacted with alarm when she suggested a flat: "…I was very surprised to hear you are looking at flats. I hope you are looking at them only to live in them till you find a home in the country for I know you would not like London and I should hate it…"

The thought of spending his precious holidays away from home depressed him and he begged his mother, "Do stop at Rooksnest [sic] for the holidays for though they would be very pleasant anyway they would not be nearly so nice if you were always looking after furniture and settling tradesmen…

34. The Grange, Stevenage, where Morgan was at school for a few unhappy weeks.

95

They would hardly be holidays at all." After a while Mrs Forster talked less about moving and seemed so engrossed with her Stevenage friends that Morgan began to hope that perhaps, after all, they would stay. He had not got over the shock as well as Mrs Forster believed, but his grief at the thought of losing his home was partly disguised by his general unhappiness at school.

Ironically, while Morgan's last three years at Rooks Nest were clouded, Mrs Forster was much happier there. The Poston family had quite taken her under their wing and she was often at Highfield, as she told Morgan: "...I hope to see a good deal of the Postons this week, May had a very bad cold. I went twice to tea and with them to the Ambulance lecture and saw Mrs P. to make [sic] a poultice and a sick bed. I was so sorry for the little boy who was performed upon but he did not seem to mind and liked his sixpence..." A little later she wrote, "...I went to the Postons yesterday and I stayed to supper and had some nice tennis..."

Morgan was so glad to be home, safe from the torments of school, that he hardly noticed how limited his environment was. His mother's comments on the doings of the neighbourhood amused him; her wit was as sharp as ever and one of her chief pleasures was talking about other people. She had caused quite a stir among her family when she gave them the news that Margaret (Daisy) Jowitt, second daughter of the Rector, had become engaged to her near neighbour, Admiral Fellowes. The "scandal" lay in the fact that the first Mrs Fellowes, who was deeply mourned in the town, had died only six months previously. She had been fifty-two when she died and Daisy was only twenty-one. When she heard of the engagement Morgan's grandmother, Mrs Whichelo, wrote to her daughter: "Good gracious! How terrible...I know I shall not get any sleep for thinking of her - she is too shocking. Why I would not have had him - much too old." In spite of her disapproval she was eager to hear more, asking her daughter in another letter, "Will Daisy be married in Stevenage by her father? You must tell me all particulars - " The gossip and speculation continued until the couple were indeed married in the parish church by the

96

Rector, after which they settled down at Woodfield, the Admiral's house opposite the Rectory and both continued with their numerous charitable works.

Now considered old enough to stay away from home without his mother, Morgan went in August 1892 for a holiday with his father's sister, Laura Forster, at West Hackhurst in Surrey. The visit was successful on the whole, although there were one or two disconcerting incidents. In her anxiety to keep Morgan amused, Aunt Laura invited the Hughes boys, sons of friends, to keep him company. One day they and Morgan were out in the donkey cart when "a reckless butcher's man" drove into it. The shafts were broken and the occupants thrown out, but fortunately there were no serious injuries. Morgan fared worst, with a badly bruised right elbow. He was very worried about telling his mother, in case she should be upset, so Aunt Laura wrote first, to explain. When Morgan did write, he pointed out to Mrs Forster that on this occasion his bad handwriting could be excused, ending his letter, "I remain Your unfortunate (not awkward) son Morgan Love to all."

In spite of "a very successful picnic at the Silent Pool" with ginger beer and buns, Morgan did not really enjoy the company of the Hughes boys. They were too rough for him and too mischievous for Aunt Laura, having broken her hammock, damaged a water barrow and stolen all the matches in the house. Morgan was glad to get back to Rooks Nest, spending as much time as possible out in the

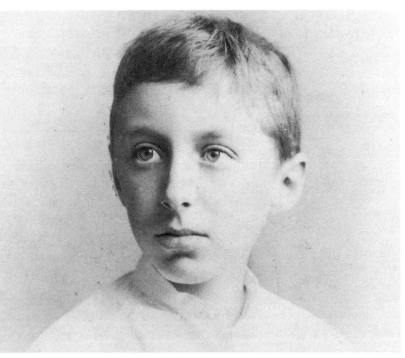

35. Morgan, aged about twelve

97

countryside with his butterfly net, away from the domestic upheaval in the house, where his mother was still superintending cleaning and redecoration work, and making intermittent attempts to find another house. It was all very disturbing for Morgan, who clung to the hope that they might stay after all.

The final blow fell with a startling suddenness in the spring of 1893. The Poyntz-Stewarts, weary of Mrs Forster's inability to make up her mind whether or not she was leaving, settled it for her by informing her that her tenancy was at an end. She was most indignant, as was her mother, who wrote vengefully: "Recollect Lily dear, not one blind or roller *to be left* unless they are *bought.* I will tear them to pieces before they shall reap the benefit of anything I have done. I am glad you have not told Morgan, it might have worried him - it will be delightful to shake yourself free *from all* but Mrs Poston and Mrs Jowitt - Rooks Nest I have always loved! Never shall we see such a sweet place..."

The truth could not be kept from Morgan for long. Now that the thing he dreaded had come to pass he set himself resolutely to look to the future, which promised in some ways to be better than he had anticipated. His mother, at last realising that boarding school did not suit her son, had decided to move to Tonbridge in Kent, so that he could attend Tonbridge School as a day-boy. Events now moved swiftly. In the summer of 1893, when the fields were full of the scent of hay, Morgan turned his back on the birdsong, the wild flowers and the pure air of Rooks Nest and was driven for the last time past the farmland bordering the Weston Road, past the Avenue and the Bowling Green, to Stevenage station, whence he was borne away to the unknown.

36. Morgan's sketch plan of Rooks Nest House and garden.

98

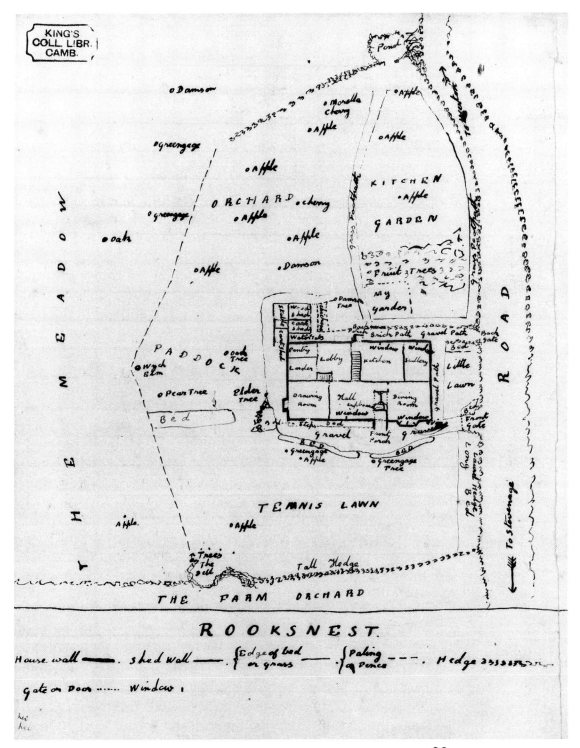

o Damson

o Morella cherry

o Apple

o greengage

r Apple

o Apple

o Apple

o Apple

ORCHARD
o cherry

o greengage
o Apple

KITCHEN
o Apple

GARDEN

o oak

o Apple

o Apple

Fruit Trees

o Damson

Nly garden

Damson Tree

Wood shed

Coal shed

Water closet

Porch Brick Path Gravel Path

Back gate

Pantry

Larder Lobby

kitchen

Window

Window

Bed

scullery

PADDOCK

o Oak Tree

Little

Lawn

o wych Elm

o Pear Tree

Elder Tree

Drawing Room

Hall
cupboard
Window

Dining Room

Bed

Front Gate

Bed

Steps

Bed

Window

Front Porch

Gravel

THE   MEADOW

Gravel

gravel

BED

o Greengage
o Apple

BED

o Greengage
Tree

Long paved Bed Hedge

TENNIS LAWN

o Apple.

o Apple

Trees
The Well

Tall Hedge

THE   FARM   ORCHARD

R O A D

To Stevenage

R O O K S N E S T.

House wall ━━━ shed Wall ━━ { Edge of bed or grass ━━ { Paling or Fence - - - Hedge ӡӡӡӡӡ

Gate or Door ⋯⋯ Window ▯

7
INTERLUDE

Once the Forsters had left, Rooks Nest was let to a succession of tenants, none of whom stayed very long. The Poyntz-Stewarts made one or two improvements, most notably the addition of a bay window in the drawing room, to the right of the fireplace. This gave the room more light as well as providing a pleasant view across the meadow.

By now there was no doubt that Niel Poyntz-Stewart was sub-normal. One of his characteristics was the repetition of all his utterances three times - "Good morning, Good morning, Good morning" - and he also had a rather curious way of moving, bent forward, half running. He was harmless, with the manners of "a perfect gentleman" but he was apt to startle people who were not used to him. The tragedy of their only son's affliction was a life-long sorrow to Charles and Caroline, to whom money and status did not bring happiness. Niel would never be able to lead an independent life, nor would there be grandchildren to inherit the Chesfield estate. But the Poyntz-Stewarts did their best to contribute to society, as their position demanded. Charles was a Justice of the Peace, a member of the Local Board and subsequently of its successor, the Stevenage Urban District Council, while Caroline was involved with charitable and church work. As wealthy landowners, the Poyntz-Stewarts wielded considerable power over the lives of ordinary people. They were respected - women curtsied and men touched their forelocks in deferential salute - but they were not loved.

At Highfield, where Morgan and his mother had spent many happy times, there was sadness when, in 1900, Mrs Poston died, much mourned by her family and friends. The servants, too, had their troubles. Emma, the long-suffering maid who had featured in so many of Mrs Forster's letters, became an unmarried mother in 1894. At this time, when illegitimacy was considered shameful, life could be very hard for both mother and child. A member of Emma's family wrote to Mrs Forster, perhaps in the hope that she would help financially:

"Madam
I right to inform you Emma Dickens as a baby by Edward Bible. I thought I would let you no.
Yours obedient Jane Dickens"

So life went forward in Stevenage. At the Rectory the Jowitt girls were marrying and leaving home. Their brother William, who had grown up to be exceptionally handsome, was at the beginning of a brilliant career in law. In 1909, three years after taking a first class honours degree in jurisprudence at Oxford, he was called to the bar and was now establishing himself as one of the most promising young men of his profession. At neighbouring Woodfield, Lord (previously Admiral) Fellowes and his wife, the former Daisy Jowitt, were happily bringing up their family of four boys, much to the delight of local people who held them in great affection.

For Morgan, the year 1897 had marked the beginning of a new life. His schooldays at Tonbridge over, he went up to King's College, Cambridge, where he discovered that happiness was at last within his reach. After years of loneliness he now found true friendship and the opportunity to exercise his intellectual powers. His novel *The Longest Journey*, published in 1907, gives a voice to his own experience as an undergraduate:

37.
Charles Poyntz-Stewart

101

INTERLUDE

"Cambridge…had taken and soothed him, and warmed him, and had laughed at him a little, saying that he must not be so tragic yet awhile, for his boyhood had been but a dusty corridor that led to the spacious halls of youth. In one year he had made many friends and learnt much…"

Early in his first term at King's, Morgan sent Maimie a postcard, describing his new way of life:

"Dear Maimie,

I will tell you my day. At 8am I go to chapel, or if I do not go I have to sign my name in a book at that time. Then I have breakfast and work from 9 to 1, when I have luncheon. Then I go for a ride, and when I come back I potter about or shop. Then sometimes I go to chapel from 5-6 and then I work from 6-7 when I have hall. After that I sometimes go out and have coffee with friends or they come to me."

As if an echo from his childhood letters, he added a comment that his sore throat was better, and concluded with a twinge of home-sickness: "I am very happy, but in spite of friends and amusements it is a great change from home."

Morgan was at Cambridge at the time of the Boer War and, like most of his compatriots, he followed the newspaper reports closely. After nationwide anxiety for the besieged garrison at Ladysmith there was general rejoicing when relief came. Morgan shared his delight with Maimie:

"I have been meaning to write to you for some time and couldn't find a better occasion than this joyful morning. The news of the relief of Ladysmith has just arrived - brought to me by the radiant bedmaker and I have rushed out to see the crowds and flags and hear the bells - especially our own chapel one, which has rung a joggly peal all by itself. I do hope the end of the war is in sight now."

After university, thanks largely to Aunt Monie's legacy, Morgan was able to indulge his desire to travel. He went first, with his mother, to Italy. On his return he spent some months teaching at the Working Men's College in London, before going, in 1905, to Germany, where he took up the post of tutor to the children of Elizabeth, Countess of Arnim. He enjoyed his time there, and admired his employer, who was later to win fame for her book *Elizabeth and her German Garden*.

102

While at university, Morgan had begun writing seriously, achieving some success with short stories. Now he launched into novels; his first, *Where Angels Fear to Tread*, was published in 1905 followed by *The Longest Journey* in 1907 and *A Room with a View* in 1908. All three were well received by the critics and Morgan's literary future seemed assured.

With such success at so early an age - *Where Angels Fear to Tread* was published when he was twenty-six - it would have been understandable if Morgan's childhood at Rooks Nest was by now relegated to the dim recesses of his mind. His next novel declared that this was far from the case. *Howards End*, published in 1910, drew together his memories of Rooks Nest, his experiences as a teacher in London and the personal beliefs he had developed during his life. The novel fused these elements together into one entity, the entity expressed in his famous "only connect."

Howards End was an instant success. It was praised by the critics as a novel about the importance of personal relationships, as a judgement on the "condition of England," as the fulfilment of the writer's early promise. It is each of these, but most of all it is an acknowledgement of Morgan's devotion to Rooks Nest and the continuing influence of his childhood days. The novel uses the house to symbolise an England whose future awaits the outcome of a deadly battle between the forces of materialism and those of the spirit.

When he began writing *Howards End*, Morgan called Stevenage "Stigansfield" which is very similar to its Anglo-Saxon name of Stigenace, but later he changed it to "Hilton." The suggestion has been made that this may be a contraction of "Hill-Town" in recognition of the Six Hills on the outskirts of the village, which so fascinated the young Morgan. He gives them considerable significance in the novel. Except for its change of name, Stevenage is not disguised in any way. Morgan faithfully depicts the Bowling Green, the dusty High Street, the old parish church of St. Nicholas, and the surrounding countryside, exactly as they were when he lived here. The Avenue, always a favourite place, is given special mention:

INTERLUDE

"Walking straight up from the station, she crossed the village green and entered the long chestnut avenue that connects it with the church. The church itself stood in the village once. But it there attracted so many worshippers that the Devil, in a pet, snatched it from its foundations, and poised it on an inconvenient knoll, three-quarters of a mile away. If this story is true, the chestnut avenue must have been planted by the angels. No more tempting approach could be imagined for the lukewarm Christian..."

Other local places which he visited, or heard of as a boy, are mentioned in *Howards End*. In chapter 41 he writes of "the house of a hermit," a reference to James Lucas, the hermit of Redcoats Green on the outskirts of Stevenage, whom Dickens once visited. Morgan could not have met him, as he died in 1874, but he may have been taken to see his desolate house. The acquisitiveness of Colonel Wilkinson and the Poyntz-Stewarts of Chesfield Park is indicated in chapter 24. They are referred to as "the people at the Park" who had taken over most of the land for miles around, including the open strip below Howards End known as the Common, as indeed happened in reality. "Landlords are horrible," declares Morgan's heroine, Margaret Schlegel, in chapter 10.

Morgan planned his novel to show the necessity for balance and connection between life's extremes; between poetry and prose, sentiment and business, femininity and masculinity. He based Margaret and Helen Schlegel, who characterise the poetic, affectionate, feminine attributes, on the Dickinson sisters whom he had met in London when he became friendly with their brother, Goldsworthy Lowes Dickinson. As a contrast, he wanted to describe a family that was dominated by down-to-earth, business-like, masculine attitudes. Limited as he was by the narrow range of his childhood acquaintance, he turned his thoughts to the Postons of Highfield, the family he knew best when he lived at Rooks Nest. It required little effort of the imagination on his part to install them at Howards End and give them the name of Wilcox, possibly a derivative of Wilkinson. He was not very inventive about names in his books, freely giving the names of living people to his characters, sometimes even attributing similar physical features to them. Both Mr Poston

104

and his son were called Charles and Morgan had no inhibitions about giving the same name to Mr Wilcox's unpleasant elder son in *Howards End*.

While Morgan's imaginative genius was at work, in real life at Highfield Charles Poston had married a young and beautiful second wife, the former Miss Clementine Brockner Bewley from Wiltshire. In 1905 their first child, Elizabeth, was born followed in 1908 by a son, Ralph.

Remembering how he had admired the Postons for their apparent confidence and self-assurance, Morgan describes the Wilcoxes of his novel as "so competent" and as having "their hands on the ropes of life." But his admiration was tinged with hostility because the Postons had different values from his; like the Wilcoxes in chapter 9 they "talked sport and politics." Mrs Wilcox, that elusive character on whom the whole book depends, was not of the same mould as the rest of the family. Morgan made her a Quaker, emphasising her difference from other mortals in her search for the "inner light." The inspiration for her character may have occurred one summer's day in 1906, when Morgan made an unexpected visit to Highfield. Clementine Poston later described the incident to her daughter Elizabeth who, realising its significance, included it in her family notes:

38. The Poston family in 1910

"A little before the guests' arrival, Clementine had gone into the rose garden. She was wearing a sweeping blue gown. It was hay time, and on that dazzling day of sun and scent and flowers, she paused to pick a handful of new mown grass for my rabbits. Looking over into the parkland, she saw a tall gangling young man in ill-fitting tweeds... 'My name is Morgan Forster.' My mother welcomed him with her ravishing smile. 'Of course, you're an old friend,' she said. 'Come along in and have lunch.' And so he joined the party on the lawn. Was it quite

INTERLUDE

by chance that Mrs Wilcox makes her first appearance in a long frock, carrying a wisp of hay?"

In calling the novel and its eponymous house *Howards End*, Morgan believed that he had invented the name by chance. The story is told of his considerable shock when he discovered later that his old home had, for at least three hundred years before he came there, been known as "Mr Howard's."

Firmly established in the literary world, Morgan associated with leading intellectuals of the day, including Virginia and Leonard Woolf, Vanessa Bell, Maynard Keynes, Roger Fry and others who were part of the circle known as the Bloomsbury Group. Their central concerns - the importance of human relationships, intellectual honesty, personal integrity, social reform - were dear to Morgan. But he was never completely subsumed by them, always maintaining a slight distance and pursuing his own individual course. His affection for his old home remained strong, nurtured by links with the Franklins. He was kept in touch with family events, such as Frank's marriage in 1907, when he sent a wedding present.

39. Terrace and lawns at Highfield

For the Postons these were happy years, enjoyed in typical Edwardian country house style. The Highfield gardens, locally renowned for their specimen trees, were a particular interest of Charles Poston. For little Elizabeth, an intense awareness of sounds was beginning to take over her life. She noticed the rhythm of her mother's heartbeat, listened to the hum of bees and asserted that she could hear earthworms moving in the soil. Dinner parties included interesting guests such as George Bernard Shaw from his home at Shaw's Corner, Ayot St. Lawrence, a dozen miles away. Elizabeth was never to forget how, as a very small girl, she crawled under the table and sat in a forest of men's trousered legs, listening to the conversation overhead. Among local friends, a special favourite of Elizabeth was Rector Jowitt who, in spite of his advancing years, would get down on all fours so that his ruddy face was on a level with the child's. Another vivid memory was the occasion when a "New Woman" - possibly one of the Strachey family - came to dinner, only to sit staring silently at the other guests. When her father commented on this to mutual friends, he was told, "Oh, don't worry. When she stares at you she is thinking about putting you in one of her books." Charles

40. Highfield as it was in 1913

INTERLUDE Poston was considerably annoyed and said that she need not come again unless she was prepared to give her hosts "the *pleasure* of her company."

All too soon tragedy struck again when, in 1913, Charles Poston died. He was buried in St. Nicholas' churchyard, close by the grave of his old friend, Rector Jowitt, who predeceased him by a year. Shortly before Charles died he had been out on a drive with his wife and they chanced to pass Rooks Nest. Suddenly, he said, "If anything should happen to me, that is where I should like to think of you." The following year the house unexpectedly became vacant and the young widow, with her eight year old daughter Elizabeth and her little son Ralph, moved into Rooks Nest.

For Elizabeth, the move was at first something of a disappointment. She observed that the fruit growing in the garden of their new home was not as good as that which they had left behind at Highfield and, of course, the house itself was smaller and not so well appointed. But very quickly she, like Morgan before her, fell in love with Rooks Nest and settled into her new life with enjoyment. She and her brother were much more free than their predecessor, being allowed to roam the fields and woods almost without restriction, either on foot or on horseback.

The young Postons were a familiar sight in the Stevenage district; Elizabeth with her dark curls and lively, outgoing personality and Ralph, fair-haired and mischievous. They took part enthusiastically in local activities: church-going, when Elizabeth would run along the grassy bank by St. Nicholas' lychgate, her Sunday boots brushing the violets which bloomed there each spring; fetes and garden parties; annual visits to the fair, eagerly awaited, for which their friend James Flack would rummage in his pockets and find them a shilling to spend on the roundabouts.

These were the war years. The Postons' arrival at Rooks Nest had coincided with the outbreak of the First World War, the impact of which was now evident all around them. In the north Hertfordshire villages and throughout the country young men were volunteering in droves to join the armed forces, in response to an unprecedented propaganda

108

campaign. At Rooks Nest Farm, Frank Franklin, now the father of four children and immune from conscription because of his job, was hard at work on the land, producing much needed food for a besieged nation. And everywhere, after the first incredible euphoria at the prospect of a just war, which would "be over by Christmas" families adjusted to the reality of daily gnawing anxiety for their sons on the battlefields of Europe.

To Morgan, the war was abhorrent. He was one of the comparatively small number who saw clearly through the intense, jingoistic patriotism of the national newspapers to the inevitable horrors beyond. Some of the literary friends who shared his views took the extremely unpopular step of becoming Conscientious Objectors. In his own family, Maimie's attitude, surprisingly in view of her past gentleness, reflected the general consensus of public opinion. Referring to an item of news in 1914, she wrote fiercely to Mrs Forster: "Did you see the Red Indians have offered to kill every German within 40 miles of them? I wish they had done it without asking permission."

Faced with such conflicting opinions among the people who meant most to him, Morgan as always made up his own mind. In November 1915 he was accepted by the International Red Cross and sent to Alexandria where he worked for the rest of the war with injured and dying soldiers, gathering information for official reports or to send home to their families. This often distressing work helped to make the lives of those concerned endurable.

Before he left for Egypt, Morgan stayed briefly at a guest house near Pulborough, in Sussex, where he wrote in the visitors' book a short prose meditation, undiscovered and unpublished until now:

"The water crept over the mud-flats towards the gorse and the blackened heather. Branksea Island lost its immense foreshore, and became a sombre episode of trees. Frome was forced inward towards Dorchester, Stow against Wimborne, Avon towards Salisbury, and over the immense displacement the sun presided, leading it to triumph ere he sank to rest. England was alive, throbbing through all her estuaries, crying for joy through the mouths of all her gulls, and the north wind, with contrary motion,

INTERLUDE

blew stronger against her rising seas. What did it mean? For what end are her fair complexities, her changes of soil, her sinuous coast? Does she belong to those who have moulded her and made her feared by other lands, or to those who have added nothing to her power, but have somehow seen her, seen the whole island at once, lying as a jewel in a silver sea, sailing as a ship of souls, with all the brave world's fleet accompanying her towards eternity? E.M. Forster.11/2/15"

Despite Morgan's lyrical prose, the reality of England for many urban dwellers in 1915 was hardship and deprivation, as the effects of war were added to existing poverty. For most Stevenage people the war did not bring food shortages, as it did to the cities. Many villagers kept chickens or a pig in the yard, growing their own fruit and vegetables fertilised with the manure so produced. Rooks Nest was no exception to this self-sufficiency; there were pigs in the orchard, beehives, a greenhouse, and a large kitchen garden, all presided over by Mr Watson, the gardener.

It was in 1915 that young Winifred Fairey came to Rooks Nest as parlourmaid. Her home was some two miles away, across the railway line at Fishers Green, where her father kept the Fisherman public house. Fairey, as she was always called by her employers, was very happy at Rooks Nest. She liked her attic bedroom and enjoyed her work, which included looking after bedrooms, glass and silverware, under the "very particular" but kindly eye of Clementine, whom she thought "a nice old lady." The open range and oil lamps were the responsibility of Mr Watson, whose sometimes over-generous hand with the paraffin caused it to drip down on to whatever food was on the kitchen table.

Porridge laced with paraffin remained a vivid memory for Elizabeth too. She was ten when Fairey came to Rooks Nest and the two struck up an instant friendship. "She was young and I was young, so we used to fool about," recalled Fairey (later Mrs Haggar). "Mrs Poston used to grumble but..." A sense of fun and the capacity for enjoying life to the full were characteristics which were to sustain Elizabeth throughout her life. Yet even in childhood she allowed nothing to divert her from the love of her life, music. She was taught at first by Clementine, who was herself a fine pianist. Soon Elizabeth

110

was devoting hours of every day to the grand piano which was placed first in the drawing room and later moved into the hall. Often she would be seated at the piano by eight o'clock in the morning. "She was always an early bird," Fairey remembered. For a time there were violin lessons from Phyllis Elliott, gifted wife of Clarence Elliott, the eminent plantsman whose nursery at Six Hills was a Mecca for gardeners throughout England. Then there was Madame Hatton-Edwards' academy at the Rookery in Stevenage High Street, where Elizabeth's love of dancing was given an outlet.

The isolation which had obtained at Rooks Nest in Mrs Forster's day was still a fact of life during the First World War. There was no telephone, no car and no swift communication with the outside world. The Postons kept a donkey and a pony; the latter, housed in the stables by the back door, earned his keep by pulling Clementine's gig. Everyone walked a great deal, although bicycles were becoming increasingly common. Fairey could not afford a bicycle, so on her weekly evening off and her fortnightly half day, she walked home to Fisher's Green, to be escorted back at night through the dark lanes by her father, or one of his customers. Yet life for the young Postons was very different from what it had been when Morgan lived there. Clementine's charm endeared her to the local community; she had the gift of friendship which drew people to her. Determined that Rooks Nest should not be cut off from the wider world, she arranged for a succession of foreign ladies to live in the house so that the children would learn their languages naturally.

Fairey remembered French, German and Russian visitors. "You were expected to understand what they wanted. No English was spoken. The children had to speak to them in their own language. They were very nice people, but the Russian was a bit of a Tartar." It was the Russian lady who once gave Fairey a bad fright, when she took up her early morning tea.

"She didn't answer. I said to Mrs Poston, 'Is Fraulein dead?' She said, 'I don't think so, Fairey. Go up and shake her.' Well, of course by that time I was shaking myself. It was the way she was wrapped up. She didn't go to bed like we did. She was like a cocoon, all wrapped in a black shawl." Fortunately the Russian lady survived.

Death came much closer to Fairey one day when the air raid warning sounded: "Mrs Poston said we'd better take cover, so they all went down the cellar. I wasn't going down in case the roof collapsed. I sat on the cellar steps. Four bombs just missed the house by a matter of feet. No one was hurt. The army came up to sort out the ground and Dad sent a man up on his bike to make sure we were all right." At the farm next door, the Franklins also took shelter in their cellar, among Frank's barrels of beer and the winter store of apples.

The end of the First World War heralded a time of social upheaval, but there was little outward change in Stevenage and the surrounding countryside. Some men came home and, if they were lucky, took over their old jobs on the land. Farming methods were little changed: horses still pulled ploughs, rakes or harrows over the chalky fields around Chesfield, Rooks Nest and Highfield. Fairey, now the proud owner of a bicycle, rode for mile after peaceful mile through the empty lanes. Hedgers and ditchers took up their former tasks, cattle were once more driven to Hitchin market and gradually, in spite of ominous signs of spreading urban unemployment, life in the villages and towns of North Hertfordshire returned - almost - to normal. For many families, nothing would ever be the same again. So many men from Stevenage, from Weston, from Graveley, had been killed in the war. Some families suffered almost unbearably: Lady Fellowes, the former Daisy Jowitt, who had caused such a stir in her youth, lost all four of her sons.

When the war ended, Elizabeth was thirteen. After the carefree years of childhood, she was sent to St. Margaret's School in Yorkshire. Boarding school was not altogether to her liking, especially the food. She excelled at music and languages, but mathematics was always to remain a closed book. Although not too unhappy at school, she was very homesick for Rooks Nest, missing her pony and the country life she had left behind. Once she actually managed to run away, making her way home by train, but her freedom was

112

short lived, as Clementine had firm views on the importance of school.

Perhaps the enforced absence had sharpened Elizabeth's awareness of the Hertfordshire countryside. In the school holidays she and her brother explored footpaths and bridleways, their natural curiosity leading them to investigate everything they passed, from woods, farms and chalkpits to the ruins of St. Etheldreda's Church at Chesfield, where one day they found a barn owl's nest. That night, lying in bed watching the moonlight stream through her window, Elizabeth could not get the thought of these beautiful birds out of her mind. Suddenly, she jumped up, pausing only to pull on her school bloomers and ran across the fields in her nightgown, to where the barn owls were. She managed to get home again, and back into bed without anyone in the house realising that she had gone, but on subsequent evenings she became over-confident, repeating the escapade once too often, with the inevitable result that a severe punishment ensued.

41. The ruined church of St. Etheldreda, Chesfield

More than anything, Elizabeth wanted to study music and after leaving school she went on to the Royal Academy of Music. Her genius was evident. In her teens she wrote the hauntingly beautiful *Sweet Suffolk Owl* inspired by an old manuscript she found at the back of a bookshelf in the library at Sishes. Other compositions followed rapidly at this period and in 1925, when she was only twenty, seven of her songs

113

were published. At the same time, she was gaining recognition as a pianist.

Wherever she went, Elizabeth became a focus for discriminating musicians, scholars and artists, who were attracted not only by her unique musical gifts, but also by her remarkable personality. Rooks Nest was a place of music, laughter and friendship. Young Babs and George Franklin, lured by the sounds wafting across the garden, would stand by the dividing hedge, watching Elizabeth practising at her piano. Their elder brother, Gordon, was friendly with Ralph and the two were sometimes impeded in their manly pursuits by little Doris Franklin, who tagged along faithfully. On one disastrous day she distinguished herself by falling into a pond, after which Ralph and Gordon, too frightened to take her straight home, went instead to the lodge at Chesfield, where Mrs Last, the keeper's wife, cleaned her up.

One very important friendship in Elizabeth's life was that of Vaughan Williams - Uncle Ralph - who helped her in her early career and saw her develop into the one composer who could carry forward his work of collecting and arranging English folksongs. His photograph, a little faded and battered with age, remained permanently on her mantelshelf. At this time, too, she met the brilliant, but unstable, young composer born Philip Heseltine, who called himself Peter Warlock. Musically, Elizabeth was influenced by his work; on a personal level their friendship meant much to her. He died, probably by suicide, in 1930. To the end of her life, Elizabeth kept a copy of his song cycle *The Curlew* open on her piano.

For Elizabeth, as for Morgan before her, Rooks Nest was security and solace in life's tragedies. Relations with the Poyntz-Stewart landlords were not always cordial, the house was not easy to run, nor was money plentiful, but the Postons were happy there. They sometimes had difficulty in keeping staff, since Rooks Nest was far from shops or bright lights. On a winter's evening, when darkness fell at four o'clock or earlier, the mile walk into Stevenage along the dark lane with high hedges on either side, could be daunting. As they passed the churchyard, the timid or imaginative

114

remembered all too clearly the tales of ghosts which their elders had told them. It only needed the screech of the silently flying barn owl to send them running, panic-stricken, for home. The most direct route from the church to the High Street was through the chestnut avenue which so delighted Morgan, but in the dark, as leaves rustled and branches creaked, the legend of the Great Black Dog sprang to mind and would not be brushed aside. It was all much as it had been in the Forsters' time, or the Howards' before them. Small wonder that servants, although happy enough with the Postons, were not keen on living so far from the village.

When the family was away, the loneliness of the house, surrounded as it was by farmland, became more apparent. Some maids did not relish the prospect of dark nights without the reassuring presence of their employer. To give them confidence, Doris, or another of the Franklins, would often agree to sleep in the house. Ruby Emery, who went to Rooks Nest as house-parlourmaid in 1932, was braver than some. When she and her sister were left in charge, they could not resist the temptation to try on Elizabeth's dresses. Ruby retained a vivid memory of Elizabeth at this time, dressed for London: "Hair right back, big loop earrings, moleskin coat, very tall and gracious." When at home in the summer, Elizabeth invariably wore a headscarf: "She was always in the garden, weeding or deadheading." Jim, the little terrier, was usually in attendance.

By the time Ruby arrived, Rooks Nest had acquired some modern conveniences: running water, electric light, an electric stove, but no telephone. Elizabeth now had a motor car which she drove fearlessly all over the country, sometimes taking the whole household with her. Ruby's diary recorded enjoyable excursions to London and Cambridge, as well as more local trips.

Fairey had remarked years earlier that Elizabeth loved the early morning. But she also enjoyed the luxury of staying in bed when there was no pressing reason to get up, and Ruby's memories are of an Elizabeth who lay listening to symphony concerts from the big radio in her room. It was Ruby's job to take up her breakfast, which consisted of half a grapefruit, cored and sectioned, with a cherry on top; toast; marmalade; a little pot of tea and some Kruschen salts, which were popularly believed to have invigorating properties. Sometimes Elizabeth would stay in bed all morning, until her mother called from the bottom of the stairs, "Are you getting up, my queen?"

The cook at this time was Ella Crisp who, like Ruby, came originally from Sandy in Bedfordshire. Every morning Clementine came into the kitchen to plan the day's meals with Ella. Dinner was usually at 7 o'clock, in the drawing room or, if guests were invited, in the hall, where a standard lamp with a big shade shaped like an Aladdin's hat, loomed over the company. Clementine was very kind to both Ruby and Ella, sometimes inviting the latter's parents, who lived locally, to Rooks Nest at weekends. At Christmas, there were gifts for both girls on the hall table, and a glass of sherry was brought to them.

The Postons travelled extensively during the 1930's, never forgetting to bring back presents for their staff. In 1932 they went to Tasmania, leaving Ruby and Ella to look after the house and to undertake the spring-cleaning in their absence. Although they thought nothing of walking or cycling along the dark lanes on their evenings off, Ruby and Ella were just a little nervous in the house at night, with no telephone. They banished their fears by sharing the big double bed and listening to the erratic sound of band music broadcast from a cat's whisker wireless set.

Elizabeth herself was now appearing on BBC radio quite often, playing both classical piano music and her own compositions. Fairey had left Rooks Nest in 1918, but to the end of her long life she tried never to miss one of Elizabeth's broadcasts: "If ever they gave it out that it was going to be her I was always on the dot. Because there was something about her playing... something nice and genteel." In Ruby's day Elizabeth was often in the throes of composing: "Bang, bang, bang on the piano, then to pen and paper ..."

Her interest in folksong led Elizabeth to visit Palestine where, in the company of a small party of musicians, she travelled the desert with Bedouin tribesmen. The country

116

made a powerful impression on her. She described the opalescent effect of sunset on the high mountains, followed by moonlight so beautiful that she could not sleep. So little modernised was Palestine then that the Bible could be used as an effective guide; failing that, she did what she had done throughout her life: "I just followed my nose." Very rarely did this approach fail, but she did encounter some danger when a group of nomads decided that her behaviour was highly sinister and held her prisoner. Fortunately her colleagues were able to persuade her captors that she was a harmless English eccentric who collected music rather than secrets.

Such adventures were a far cry from the tranquillity of North Hertfordshire, where the greatest excitement of summer concerned the fortunes of village cricket teams. At Chesfield, the Poyntz-Stewarts arranged for local teams to play an eleven nominally captained by Niel who could play after a fashion. According to Ruby's fiance, Ron Game, who often played at Chesfield, a great cheer went up every time Niel managed to hit the ball. The matches, played in an idyllic rural setting, were enjoyed by all who took part, as was the splendid tea in the pavilion afterwards.

The widening horizons of her musical career, counterbalanced by the demands of country life at Rooks Nest, fully absorbed Elizabeth's attention during the 1930's, but she could not escape the fact that once again war was imminent. On July 18th 1936, the Spanish Civil War erupted, capturing the imagination of young people throughout the world, not least writers, artists and intellectuals, many of whom joined in the fighting. One Englishman who enlisted with P.O.U.M. (The Workers' Party of Marxist Liberation) was George Orwell, who at this time was living at Wallington, a tiny village about ten miles north of Stevenage, where he tried to make an income by running the village shop. Although wounded, he survived the experience, which he wrote about in *Homage to Catalonia*.

The Bloomsbury Group suffered a severe loss when Julian Bell, son of Vanessa and nephew of Virginia Woolf, was killed. The brutalities of this war lingered on in the European consciousness. When she visited Spain many years afterwards, Elizabeth found it depressing, saying that it was a country so steeped in blood that she could smell it still. Yet the Spanish Civil War, with all its cruelties, was but a prelude to an even more horrible war. Morgan Forster could see only too clearly the terror that lay ahead. As early as 1935, in an article entitled *The Menace to Freedom*, he wrote:

> "The tyrant no longer appears as a freak from the pit, he is becoming the norm, country after country throws him up, he springs from any class of society with an ease which once seemed admirable; requiring only opportunity and ruthlessness, he supersedes parliaments and kings. And consequently many people do not believe in freedom any more, and the few who do regard it as something that must be discovered, not recovered."

As it became clear that a second world war was inevitable, preparations were made to provide gas-masks, ration books, bomb-shelters and all the other melancholy and frightening paraphernalia of wartime life. Hardship, danger and perhaps the ultimate horror of invasion lay ahead. Morgan had no illusions about the future, but Elizabeth, at the age of thirty-four, with a brilliant musical career ahead of her, did not at first appreciate the implications of the coming war. In 1939 she received a letter from the BBC, inviting her to join their staff. She refused - "I was so green I thought I could just stay here and write music - " but then the war came, and with it call-up papers to the Land Army. Somewhat nervously she wrote again to the BBC, saying that she had reconsidered their offer. Their reply was swift, and as the sirens wailed for the Second World War, Elizabeth Poston began her service with the BBC.

42. Elizabeth Poston in the 1930's

118

8
REUNION

"...I have to tell you now that no such undertaking has been received and that consequently this country is at war with Germany." On September 3rd 1939 these fateful words of Prime Minister Neville Chamberlain were broadcast to the British people over BBC radio. In Stevenage the Prime Minister's message was heard in resigned and gloomy silence, after which the first awful wail of the air-raid warning siren outside the fire station in Church Lane (the Back Lane of Morgan's childhood) caused a moment of panic. On this occasion it was a false alarm; in the coming months it would be all too real. Then came a time of fearful inactivity as people waited, as if in a vacuum, for the war to begin.

Meanwhile there were unaccustomed rituals to be performed, such as "the blackout" - the nightly task of putting up black curtains over windows and doors, to prevent any chink of light showing which might guide German bombers searching overhead for targets. Virtually all houses at this time were heated by open fires, whose glow could be seen through uncurtained windows. One family moving into a new house on a cold November day in 1939 tried in vain to light a first fire in the new hearth. By dusk they were still unsuccessful and, cold and tired, they went upstairs to blackout the windows. Almost immediately they were startled to hear a tremendous hammering on the front door, and an irate Air Raid Precautions Officer shouting orders to "Put out that light." The fire had decided that this was an appropriate moment to burst into flames. Such small, almost farcical, incidents were being repeated all over the country and their combined effect was to change the reality of everyday life from comparative freedom of action to the constant, unending necessity to think before doing or saying the most commonplace things.

As the war had been announced by radio, so it was to the radio that people turned for news throughout the six years of conflict. Another fixed routine in most people's lives was the nightly appointment with the BBC's nine o'clock News, after which they went to bed encouraged or depressed according to the course of events. Radio was now an essential means of communication. Although public service television had existed since 1936, it was insufficiently developed to be of general use and was suspended for the duration of the war. The press, of course, still played a vital role, but radio was the medium of the hour. It was more up-to-date than newspapers yet cheap enough for most homes to possess a receiver, although by the end of the war there were still some Stevenage families who could not afford one. Familiarly known as "the wireless", these 1940's receivers were the size of modern television sets often with poor reception as mysterious crackles and hisses disturbed the broadcast. The power source was a large battery or "accumulator" which had to be topped up with acid at frequent intervals. This could be done at, among other places, the Stevenage Motor Company opposite Holy Trinity Church in the High Street. The service was by no means instant, and customers could face several days' wait.

Wartime radio was far more than a news medium. It was used to broadcast comedy programmes such as *It's That Man Again* (ITMA) to keep the nation cheerful, and programmes on the arts and music to keep up morale. Debate and discussion, variety shows, plays, concerts, as well as vital information for farmers and others were all relayed into British homes - and abroad - through BBC radio. One effect was to bring the nation together, as everyone received the same information and shared the same anxieties. The importance of BBC radio during the war cannot be over-estimated; those who were in any way involved with it at that period were at the same time privileged and burdened. This was true of Elizabeth Poston and Morgan Forster, in both of whose wartime lives the BBC held a central position.

Early in the war, Morgan was asked to take part in a series of broadcasts to India and this he agreed to do. At first he

121

found radio a difficult medium, but he persevered, eventually developing a very effective microphone manner. His Indian broadcasts, which continued throughout the war, were mainly about books. They were very much appreciated by the Indian people and are still remembered with affection today. But Morgan was concerned that, in the early days of the war, the BBC was devoting very little time to literature for its British listeners. He made public statements deploring this state of affairs, with the result that literary items began to be included in the broadcasting schedules. With Ralph Vaughan Williams and others, he was involved in a more serious dispute, concerning the right of BBC employees and contributors to freedom of speech, a subject about which Morgan felt very strongly indeed. Thanks to his campaign, the government was persuaded to reconstitute the BBC's Board of Governors minus its two "advisors" (some called them censors) and to allow the new Board complete freedom within the law to decide on programmes and contributors.

To many people the most evil and horrible aspect of Nazism was its persecution of Jews. That a so-called civilised nation should descend to such barbarism in the modern age was beyond belief, which was partly why the full horror of events did not penetrate to the minds of ordinary British citizens until after the war. Yet already in 1939, Morgan had put the facts bluntly before them, in his essay *Jew-Consciousness*. He wrote then: "Jew-mania was the one evil which no-one foretold at the end of the last war. All sorts of troubles were discerned and discernible...But no prophet, so far as I know had seen this anti-Jew horror, whereas today no-one can see the end of it."

In 1940, Morgan went further, making three anti-Nazi broadcasts: *Culture and Freedom, What has Germany done to the Germans?* and *What would the Germans do to us?* He ended with a characteristically honest and courageous statement: "In this difficult day when so many of us are afraid it is a comfort to remember that violence has so far never worked."

Morgan had every reason to be afraid. His high profile attacks on the Nazis had resulted in his inclusion on their

122

death list. Had the German invasion taken place - and this
seemed a strong possibility in 1940 - he would have been
hunted down and destroyed. Fully aware of this, he chose to
remain in England, even though he had sufficient money
and contacts to enable him to follow the example of some
other writers who had escaped to America or Canada.

For Elizabeth Poston, life with the BBC in wartime
brought not only new friendships and exciting new
opportunities, but also frustrations, followed by unlooked-
for responsibilities. Under the chairmanship of Lord Reith
the BBC imposed very strict rules about both the content of
broadcasts and the activities of its employees. Those who
worked for the BBC were required to sign agreements not to
publish books, nor to take part in public performances except
under its auspices. Staff were expected to reserve all their
energies and their total output for the BBC. These
regulations were particularly irksome to musicians for
whom public performance was essential. If the restrictions
and shortages of wartime were difficult enough to cope with,
how much more so was this limitation on their music-
making. That was the opinion of Elizabeth when she
received an invitation from Dame Myra Hess to play the
piano at one of her famous concerts at the National Gallery.

Convinced that such an opportunity was not to be refused,
rules or no rules, Elizabeth prepared her strategy with care,
managing to elude the BBC and take her place at the piano at
the appointed hour. She was wearing evening dress and
make-up: "I was got up as glamorously as possible as
everyone did in order to cheer themselves up." At the end of
the concert a man was seen making his way diffidently across
the crowded room to where she sat, tall and beautiful, the
centre of an animated group. He said nervously, "You won't
know me - I used to live in your house - name's Forster."
Elizabeth was amazed and delighted. As they talked his
continuing affection for his childhood home became so
obvious that she said spontaneously, "Why don't you come
back with me now?" He refused then, alarmed at the
prospect of meeting Clementine, and afraid that the house
would be so changed as to shatter his mental images of it.

REUNION But curiosity won and when, not long afterwards, he took up Elizabeth's invitation, he was overjoyed to find that practically nothing had altered; house and garden were as he remembered them.

The reunion between Morgan and his childhood home brought him also the joy of new friendships. Once his initial shyness had worn off he became very happy and relaxed in Elizabeth's company and he developed a deep affection for Clementine, which she reciprocated. For the rest of his life he was a regular visitor to Rooks Nest, often coming when he felt restless or unhappy, as if to a place of sanctuary. The unchanging nature of house and countryside was a solace to him; to Elizabeth it was as if he was trying to get back to the womb.

The apparent continuity at Rooks Nest was an illusion. For people in Stevenage and the surrounding villages, life seemed to consist of rapid change alternating with dreadful monotony. The majority of able-bodied men were called up for national service in the army, navy or air force, or directed into some reserved occupation. Women were also called up, some to civilian duties such as the Land Army, others to women's branches of the fighting services. The effect on family life was disruptive. Some wives did not see their husbands, or children their fathers, for five years; some waited in dread for news from German or Japanese prisoner-of-war camps; others lived for the infrequent visits of sons who had become uniformed strangers.

Tanks appeared on the Bury Mead where, for some inexplicable reason, rolls of barbed wire were placed between the trees in the Avenue. The High Street, dark and cheerless in the nightly blackout, was alive in the day with convoys of army vehicles. Once again the Old Castle Inn opened its doors as a canteen for passing troops, as did Springfield House, now owned by local millionaire Jeremiah Inns. Many Stevenage families had been allocated evacuees from London; the Grange, where Morgan had been so bitterly unhappy, had been taken over by Hertfordshire County Council to house children from Briar Patch Children's Home, whose Letchworth premises had burned down;

124

German and Italian prisoners of war were employed on local farms; those men who were not called up joined the Home Guard, devoting much of their non-working time to training.

Less dramatic than the military activity was the shortage of everyday necessities. Ration books were allocated from the Food Office in the High Street; without them staple items of food such as meat and cheese could not be bought, even assuming they were available. Long queues at the butcher's, grocer's or baker's became a fact of life. Those who could "dug for victory" by growing their own vegetables and fruit in allotments or gardens; many had both. Clothing and furniture was also in short supply, sold only in exchange for the coupons allocated to each individual. When a young woman got married she was unlikely to have a new wedding dress unless all her friends gave her their coupons to buy material; more often than not, the wedding party would wear everyday clothes which now, for the groom, meant uniform. The quality of most manufactured items deteriorated as the importation of raw materials became increasingly difficult. To give some protection to the public, the government introduced "utility

43. Morgan at Rooks Nest House in the 1940's

125

marks" to be stamped on goods which met minimum standards of serviceability.

Rooks Nest was, of course, deeply affected by the war. Elizabeth's BBC work meant that she was away from home for much of the time, leaving her aging mother, with rapidly diminishing help, to cope with the house and grounds. At the farm, the Franklin family was heavily involved in the war effort. Babs had already enlisted in the Women's Royal Army Corps in 1938, but had not so far been sent further from home than St. Albans. When war was declared on September 3rd 1939 her mother and sister were on holiday in Scotland and her first thought was that she would be called up before they came home to say goodbye. In fact she was first billeted at Highbury Road, Hitchin, before being sent to Woolwich Arsenal where she was directed to pack ammunition, only to be thwarted by male colleagues who gallantly took over themselves - "It's too dangerous for you girls."

Gordon Franklin, Babs' brother, was commissioned in the Royal Corps of Signals before the war started, and later posted to Rheims. He followed his sister's progress with interest, intending to arrange for her to join him as an army cook. Before this could happen, he was killed at Dunkirk, as were several other young men from local families. When Babs did go abroad, in January 1943, it was to Cairo as a military policewoman. Unbeknown to her mother, who thought she had no choice in the matter, she had volunteered and been selected as one of the first six women to start the military police service abroad. Her exploits did not go unremarked: two years later the *Hertfordshire Express* ran a front page story under the headline "An ATS Provost Pioneer: Stevenage Girl's Romantic Career."

At home in Stevenage, in spite of the shortages, the restrictions and the losses, some things remained unchanged. Mrs Poyntz-Stewart still drove through the lanes in her basket-weave pony trap, often stopping at Rooks Nest Farm, remaining seated to shout, "Mr Franklin, Mr Franklin," at which he was expected to run out to do her bidding. In the same way she would proceed along the High

126

44. Morgan with Frank Franklin at Rooks Nest Farm

Street, never leaving the trap but calling for the shopkeepers to come for her orders. Niel usually followed her on his bicycle and unkind children would yell, "Look out, Niel, your back wheel's going round," at which he would unfailingly get off and look.

In October 1943, when Morgan paid one of his now frequent visits to Rooks Nest, he chanced to see Niel searching for mushrooms. The fleeting moment stayed in his mind and, coupled with a completely unrelated incident,

127

West Hackhurst.
Abinger Hammer   2 3 - 10 - 44
Dorking

Dear Frank.

I enclose some books, and I have inscribed our names in them. A Passage to India is a Yank edition, but the print and paper is better than the English edition. You will find some information in it about me — mostly wrong. I have also put in a little Service Edition of one of the other novels, and a volume of essays about Alexandria which I thought you might like to have as your daughter is in Egypt. I am very pleased to be sending the books to you.

I much enjoyed seeing you again and being in the farm. They room where we sit is one of my earliest memories and my pleasantest. I found my mother fairly well and interested in all the news. She sends her love. If all goes well, I shall be looking in before the end of the year again.

With kind wishes to all, including your little grandson.

Yours affectionately

Morgan

45. Letter to Frank Franklin **set up a train of thought about life, death and the emotions** from Morgan. **which he later wrote up in his** *Commonplace Book*:

> "Two events have made me feel lately *(i)* the sight of Neil Stuart [sic], aged 60 now, running round in the low sunshine after mushrooms at Chesfield and untouched by time *(ii)* the slim oak which nearly hit me as it was felled yesterday [not at Rooks Nest but in his garden at West Hackhurst]. Neil seemed holy, part of my childhood. Though frightened by men he moved towards us rapidly as if going to speak, then swerved. I am glad I did not speak to him. The tree might have killed me...So, this way and that, we are beckoned out of the life where we keep engagements, make points, do kindnesses, etc., into regions of emotions where we do not feel at home. My wisdom seemed loss for an instant when I saw Niel; he had been preserved from experience - which is not necessarily good or bad, but which always makes a general modification in the same direction and causes men of 60 to meet in their 60s...The tree means that great pain or death are always close in terrible freshness...the Neil Stuart emotion was strictly poetic and of the depth which de la Mare used to reach; no deeper.

128

The right words for it are unfindable, for the particular contours of the path, the particular slant of the sun..."

An idyllic walk through the fields could be interrupted, like any other activity, by the sudden howl of the air raid warning siren. Taking cover in a ditch, or under a hedge, walkers would gaze cautiously at the sky, holding their breath as German planes flew low enough for their swastika markings to be clearly visible. Stevenage and North Hertfordshire did not entirely escape these bombing raids, but in comparison with the sufferings of London and other major cities, they were fortunate. As the London Blitz intensified, not only children, but also organisations and businesses, were moved out of the city to the comparative safety of the countryside. The BBC was one of these; its specialist services were grouped into divisions, to be relocated in various towns across England.

BBC Music was sent for a time to Bedford, and with it Elizabeth Poston, an unenthusiastic evacuee. Once established in "dreary digs", she soon discovered that there was nowhere to go in the evenings and often nothing to do from six o'clock onwards. Since her unwilling hosts, who did not even provide a chair in her room, made it clear that she was not welcome, she and a colleague often resorted to taking long walks in the dark as the only way of keeping warm and occupied. Sometimes they walked out of Bedford, into the flat countryside beyond, searching for a public house that might offer warmth and a place to sit. On one occasion in mid-winter they found refuge from the snow-bound countryside in front of a roaring pub fire, and spent the whole evening dozing in the unaccustomed heat. When "time" was called, Elizabeth woke with a start to a horrible smell and the discovery that the soles of her boots had burned through. She never forgot the walk back through the snow.

A variety of calamities lay in wait for the unwary night walkers. One expedition ended in chaos when, on their way home, they fell into a booby-trapped protective trench dug by the Home Guard. A warning device exploded, causing agitated Home Guard troops to erupt from all directions.

129

REUNION   Such an incident would normally have been dealt with severely but, according to Elizabeth's modest interpretation of events, the BBC was by then very short of staff and the matter was overlooked.

Not only was food and clothing rationed, but also petrol. Comparatively few people had cars at this time but even so, such was the difficulty of maintaining oil supplies, that it was found necessary to restrict very severely the amount of petrol allocated to private individuals. While she was stationed at Bedford Elizabeth did occasionally manage to save up a sufficient supply to enable her to get home to Rooks Nest. Sometimes, to provide a welcome break from the monotony of life in digs, she would take with her a colleague who was not so fortunately placed. The road from Bedford to Stevenage was nearly empty of traffic, except for RAF vehicles at Cardington and those from the United States Air Force base at Chicksands. American troops, who apparently found their evenings as tedious as did the BBC staff, made a habit of coming into Bedford to patronise the town pubs. Every night, declared Elizabeth, the churchyard of St. Paul's was full of drunken Americans asleep on the tombs.

It was from St. Paul's church that the BBC broadcast its music programmes. A large notice on the door instructed "DO NOT ENTER IN HOME GUARD BOOTS." The intention was to protect the tiled floor but, as most men wore boots constantly, little attention was paid to the order and BBC microphones often picked up the sound of late choir members clattering across the floor, followed by the inevitable crash as one slipped over. Elizabeth always feared that the listening public would think the broadcasts were taking place in the midst of a bombardment.

The bicycle has long been a favourite mode of transport in Bedford and was particularly so during the war when petrol was scarce. BBC staff found it useful to have their own bicycles, but even this innocuous activity was fraught with danger. The BBC conductor and Director of Music was Sir Adrian Boult. He was an exceptionally tall man and a standard bicycle was no use to him, so he had a specially

130

large one built, with a container in front somewhat like a delivery boy's basket, to hold his music. It was not long before several complaints were received from local residents who said that he was so high up that he could see into their bedroom windows as he rode by. Horrified to think that he had given offence, he at once gave up his bicycle and went about the town on foot.

Another distinguished Doctor of Music also came to grief on a bicycle. He had a devoted secretary who always cycled a respectful few feet behind him and they were often observed proceeding through Bedford in this fashion. One pitch dark night they were pedalling towards a river bridge which was devoid of its railings since they had been commandeered, like most other removable metal objects, for making armaments. The doctor rode straight into the river followed, at the appropriate interval, by his secretary. Fortunately the mud of the shallows converted a potential tragedy into farce, to the delight of all who heard it. Humour helped people survive the awfulness of war; Elizabeth was particularly blessed in this respect, and could usually kindle a spark of amusement even at her darkest moments.

The harsh realities of war were thrust in front of Elizabeth when she was recalled to London, to undertake new duties for the BBC at Bush House. Here she did secret service work, carrying out an idea thought to have been originated by Churchill, whereby gramophone records were used to broadcast coded messages to resistance movements in Europe. Although she received instructions from a superior, she was the only person actually to operate the system. It was a nerve-racking business; if she had played a wrong tune, she could have caused the people of some Nazi-occupied country to rise against their oppressors too soon, to meet certain destruction. To the end of her life she had recurrent nightmares in which this happened.

As well as her responsibility for the musical codes, Elizabeth had the task of interviewing refugees and escapees, helping them to send messages of hope to their families at home through the direct telephone links to occupied countries such as Yugoslavia, which were kept open all through the war. It was often difficult to get the men to talk naturally, but she found that if she could persuade them to sing, perhaps a local folksong, it convinced their relatives since these were virtually impossible to fake.

Elizabeth found the refugees' testimonies pathetic and moving. One man who was brought to her office had escaped capture by swimming through icy water. When she offered him a cigarette he was embarrassed, and put his hands behind his back, while her secretaries made frantic but incomprehensible signals to her. The man's desperate plunge for freedom had caused frostbite, resulting in the loss of his fingers. When Elizabeth realised this she acted with typical swiftness and sensitivity, by immediately placing the cigarette in her lips and allowing him to take it in his.

A happier incident concerned some French sailors who had arrived at Bristol, but could not be persuaded to talk or sing. Elizabeth was sent with Douglas Cleverdon to interview them, but failed to elicit any response. Finally, they were inspired to buy sherry and press it upon the sailors, who drank it with enthusiasm and burst into song. Elizabeth's expenses sheet for the day included a claim for "bottles of sherry to make Frenchmen sing."

In 1944, as a final assault on British towns and cities, the Germans began dispatching their sinister V2 flying bombs. Stevenage was largely unscathed, but a number of these instruments of destruction landed near the Forsters' home at Abinger Hammer in Surrey. Morgan remarked on the calm manner in which he and his mother, who was now eighty-eight, went about their daily lives. He felt almost ashamed at the speed with which they had adapted to this new danger, although he believed that the V2's, which seemed to drop at random from a clear sky, would have an important psychological impact on the war-weary people of Britain.

From the first London Blitz in 1940 it was plain that the resulting devastation would present an immense problem after the war. As an act of hope during the most depressing months, the government commissioned a range of reports and proposals suggesting ways in which to achieve the "post-war reconstruction" which would so obviously be necessary.

One of those most active in this work was William Jowitt who, having been readmitted to the Labour Party in 1936, was returned to Parliament in 1939, appointed Solicitor-General in 1940, Attorney-General in 1942, Minister-without-Portfolio in 1943 and Minister for National Insurance in 1944. It was in 1944, too, that Sir Patrick Abercrombie presented his Greater London Plan, which proposed that a series of new towns be established, each accommodating 60,000 to 80,000 people from the overcrowded capital, sited on a radius of 25 to 30 miles from London. Apart from those directly involved, no one paid much attention to such proposals at the time. Life was too exhausting for most people to think much about the future; they were fully occupied with the exigencies of surviving the present.

There was, however, a general wish that life for all sections of society should be better in that elusive time "after the war." Many realised that this would not be achieved easily; there would be major philosophical and political issues to be addressed, as well as practical readjustments. Morgan saw this clearly. When he was asked by the Crown Film Unit to contribute a film script on the theme of the future, he wrote *A Diary for Timothy*. In this thought-provoking, beautifully evocative short film, made in 1945, he is true to his vision of "only connect." Deliberately including music by Beethoven, he makes the point that, for many people, this is the most beautiful music ever written and yet it was composed by a German. The film ends with the daunting question, "Are you going to make the world a different place? You and the other babies?"

46. Kitchen Garden at Rooks Nest House

9
THE FORSTER COUNTRY CAMPAIGNS

With the ending of the Second World War Stevenage, like many another country town, looked forward to peace and a better way of life. For some families, nothing could ever be the same again; theirs were the names to be added to the War Memorial on the Bowling Green. For others, the full horrors of the war were only now becoming clear as men returning from abroad told their grim stories. The Revd. John King, brother-in-law of Elizabeth Poston, was appointed Rector of Stevenage in December 1945. He had been in a German prison camp for five years, and he was later joined by a curate, the Revd. Ted Harper, who had been a Japanese prisoner. They and others like them, were living witnesses to the brutality of war, and of the need for a future founded on humane values.

1945 found many people exhausted, not least Elizabeth Poston, whose stressful years at the BBC had left her physically and mentally drained. The breakdown which followed was a time of complete forgetfulness, as her exhausted mind blanked out. Looking back later, she remembered only lying on a seat in the garden, while her mother sustained her with trays of food. She could not at first decide what to do about a job, since, in her words, "Secret Service agent was no basis for a new career." The BBC gave her sick-leave, but she decided to resign, in order to continue her own work, which included taking up an opportunity to go to America and Canada. Here she began researching the folksongs and jazz which were later to form the basis of her *Penguin Book of American Folksongs*. On her return she made up her mind to do freelance work from Rooks Nest, since managing the house alone was becoming too much for her elderly mother.

Morgan also travelled abroad for the first time for many years when, in October 1945, he went to a writers' conference in India, at the request of the All-India PEN. The visit was timely, in that it helped to take his mind off the recent death of his mother, but while he was away Lady Bridges, owner of his rented house at West Hackhurst, wrote giving notice that his lease would be terminated in a year's time, as she wanted the house for a relative. He had lived there for twenty-two years, and the prospect of looking for another home at the age of sixty-six was daunting. In his biography of Forster, P.N. Furbank states: "He began to consider where he might go when he left Abinger. His first thought was Stevenage, his childhood home and the place where, if anywhere, he could imagine he had roots."

But Stevenage was in turmoil. Determined to do something on a grand scale to meet the desperate need of the many thousands in London who had been made homeless by the war, the Labour government had set up a Ministry of Town and Country Planning which, headed by Lewis Silkin, decided to build a ring of modern, well-planned "satellite towns" on a thirty mile radius from London. Stevenage, with its excellent road and rail links, was to be the first of these. The concept of "new towns" was revolutionary, an unknown quantity; many local people did not fully understand what was happening and, with hindsight, it is doubtful if all the planners did either. To a large extent Stevenage was being used as a guinea pig and the experience was painful, not least because most people were racked by conflicting emotions. Stevenage residents knew something about the sufferings of London; they had taken in evacuees and heard first-hand accounts of the horrors of the Blitz; many had relatives or friends in London; local firemen had gone to the assistance of the blazing capital; some older men travelled daily to work there and were themselves bombed out of factories and offices. There was no lack of feeling for the London homeless. The bitterness and even hatred which now erupted was directed at planners and bureaucrats.

In both Morgan Forster and Elizabeth Poston the conflict was acute. Both had witnessed suffering during the war and

135

THE FORSTER COUNTRY CAMPAIGNS

had done what they could in practical ways to alleviate it; both were compassionate; both believed in breaking down barriers between people. For Morgan, the turn of events was particularly disturbing since, as a matter of principle, he voted Socialist. But there are two sides to every question. For Elizabeth there was no doubt that the local people whose homes were about to be bulldozed, whose fields and gardens would disappear under concrete, must be helped; and, overriding every other consideration, as much as possible of the gentle Hertfordshire countryside, with its rich variety of wildlife, must be saved.

Furious activity now overtook Stevenage and Elizabeth, with various members of the Franklin family and others, was in the midst of it. They appealed to Morgan for help and he, horrified at the scale of the destruction about to descend upon the village and countryside which had always seemed to him to epitomise England, agreed to support their campaign. He sent Elizabeth an encouraging postcard from West Hackhurst:

"Friday, W.H.

"I left parcel at BBC about 5.0 yesterday. Heard you had already called. Hope you called again and found it, and that it is helpful. Please let me know how things go. Also please find me a house! EMF"

The irony of his approaching homelessness in view of the current furore over the satellite town proposal is unlikely to have been lost on Morgan. His own housing problem was solved when he was made an Honorary Fellow of Kings College, Cambridge and offered rooms there. But he had committed himself to the campaign to save the Stevenage countryside. Never afraid to speak out on behalf of a cause which he believed in, he took the opportunity, when invited by the BBC to contribute to a series of programmes entitled *The Challenge of Our Time*, to make a public statement. In May 1946 he gave the famous broadcast in which he clarified his own position:

"I belong to the fag-end of Victorian liberalism, and can look back to an age whose challenges were moderate in their tone...In many ways it was an admirable age. It practised benevolence and philanthropy, was humane and intellectually curious, upheld free

136

speech, had little colour-prejudice, believed that individuals are and should be different...The education I received in those far-off and fantastic days made me soft, and I am very glad it did...But though the education was humane it was imperfect, inasmuch as we none of us realised our economic position. In came the nice fat dividends, up rose the lofty thoughts, and we did not realise that all the time we were exploiting the poor of our own country and the backward races abroad, and getting bigger profits from our investments than we should...

All that has changed in the present century. The dividends have shrunk to decent proportions and have in some cases disappeared. The poor have kicked. The backward races are kicking - and more power to their boots..."

Clearly, Morgan's sympathies were with those who would now be described as "underprivileged" - those who were inadequately housed, underpaid, ill-nourished - and he wanted a more equal spread of the country's wealth. He realised that to bring this about would involve planning for a new economy and that, inevitably, planning would remove some freedom from the individual. Recognising that, to some extent, this reflected the age-old dichotomy of material and spiritual values, his broadcast continued:

"In a time of upheaval like the present, this collision of principles, this split in one's loyalties, is always occurring. It has just occurred in my own life. I was brought up as a boy in one of the home counties, in a district which I still think the loveliest in England. There is nothing special about it - it is agricultural land, and could not be described in terms of beauty spots. It must always have looked much the same. I have kept in touch with it, going back to it as to an abiding city and still visiting the house which was once my home, for it is occupied by friends. A farm is through the hedge, and when the farmer there was eight years old and I was nine we used to jump up and down on his grandfather's straw ricks and spoil them. Today he is a grandfather himself, so that I have the sense of five generations continuing in one place. Life went on there as usual until this spring. Then someone who was applying for a permit to lay a water-pipe was casually informed that it would not be granted since the whole area had been commandeered. Commandeered for what? Had not the war ended? Appropriate officials of the Ministry of Town and Country Planning now arrived from London and announced that a satellite town for sixty thousand people is to be built. The people now living and working there are doomed; it is death in life for them and they move in a nightmare. The best agricultural land has been

137

THE FORSTER COUNTRY CAMPAIGNS

taken, they assert; the poor land down by the railway has been left; compensation is inadequate. Anyhow, the satellite town has finished them off as completely as it will obliterate the ancient and delicate scenery. Meteorite town would be a better name. It has fallen out of a blue sky.

'Well,' says the voice of planning and progress, 'why this sentimentality? People must have houses.' They must, and I think of working-class friends in north London who have to bring up four children in two rooms, and many are even worse off than that. But I cannot equate the problem. It is a collision of loyalties. I cannot free myself from the conviction that something irreplaceable has been destroyed, and that a little piece of England has died as surely as if a bomb had hit it. I wonder what compensation there is in the world of the spirit for the destruction of the life here, the life of tradition." (*Two Cheers for Democracy*, Penguin, 1975).

The broadcast aroused controversy. Correspondence in *The Listener* included an offended letter from the Ministry of Town and Country Planning, pointing out inaccurate statements in Morgan's text. After further consultation with Elizabeth, who was keeping him up-to-date with cuttings from local newspapers, he wrote to her on May 29th 1946:

"Dear Elizabeth

I return the fascinating cuttings. Mr Berry can't possibly be troubled in his private capacity. I mentioned him - and that diffidently - because I thought he might be dealing with enquiries from his office.

"I enclose a rough draft of my reply to the Town Planners. You will see that I still refuse to give the name of the place and this has the additional advantage of not involving the *Listener*; further letters might have been sent to it, I mean. I expect I shall hear more from the T.P., but only one. I am rather pleased with my last paragraph - more pleased I hope than he will be.

"I am looking forward to your visit, and so glad that you can stay a night. Am relieved that Beatrice is back. It must have been an additional strain on your mother.

With affectionate greetings to you both. Yrs. E.M.Forster"

The Mr Berry referred to in the letter was Mr Geoffrey Seager Berry, Clerk to the Stevenage Urban District Council and, incidentally, a descendant of the Revd John Lingen Seager who had owned the Grange School when Morgan was a boy. The draft reply to "the planners" ran:

"West Hackhurst, Abinger Hammer, Dorking 28-5-46
"Dear Sir

138

I have now heard from my informant, and am pleased to reply to your letter.

(i) She was incorrect in stating that 'nobody knew' of the scheme before the incident of the water-pipe. The proper phrase would have been 'scarcely anyone knew', and I regret that I did not use this in my broadcast.

ii) As regards your allusion to the 'two months' local advertisement by the promoting authority she would be glad to know under what Act this provision is made. She does not know of any such clause. She adds 'Under the New Towns Bill it is set out that one month's notice shall be given by the Minister. This he has not yet power to do until the Act is passed.' The area in question was included as a proposed site under the Abercrombie Scheme, but only recently was information received of its adoption by the government. The Council received information shortly before Easter and before the end of April notices of compulsory sale were sent out.

(iii) I deliberately omitted the name of the area from my broadcast, since I do not wish those living in it to be troubled with additional correspondence. The topic was only incidental and illustrative to my talk, the subject of which was 'The Challenge of Our Time.'

(iv) It is probable that if the people in the area had been more alert to indications they would not have had so late and so rude an awakening. The conduct of the officials concerned may well have been professionally correct. But I welcome this opportunity of pointing out that correctness is not enough. In this age of changes drastically affecting the ordinary man, it is the duty of officials not merely to advertise their plans but to bring them home to him in an appropriate form. They ought, in other words, to make a more profound and a more respectful study of local psychology than appears to have obtained in the present instance."

Many others joined the debate through the columns of both local and national newspapers. The majority were against the plans for a satellite town, but one or two spoke with an alternative voice, including the writer of this letter published in *The Hertfordshire Express* for May 11th 1946:

"Sir,

Come along Stevenage! Where is the Pioneer Reform Spirit? Where is progression? It is hard, very hard, to give up one's home, but think of the millions being pushed from pillar to post;no chance of saving for homes, not wanted in other people's homes, having to find happiness without their own four walls...Stevenage has escaped the war without a mark, but millions of people were robbed of home, furniture, their all - with little chance of their being replaced. Some will never pick up the old threads in this world as theirs was the supreme sacrifice.

Is it too much to make a sacrifice for peace? I, among many thousands, are being forced out of rooms with nowhere to go, and not much hope unless houses are built, and quickly.

The Stevenage people have been promised other homes: they will still have their personal possessions, and will have the satisfaction of knowing that they have helped in a big way to fight and co-operate for peace and progress.

A HOMELESS CITIZEN AND NATIVE OF STEVENAGE"

Sadly, but perhaps inevitably, other correspondents and the press began to join the debate from party political lines. Following one of her own letters to a local paper, Elizabeth received, on 13 May 1946, an anonymous letter whose sentiments were typical of many people who opposed the concept of satellite towns:

"We read in your letter in the newspaper that 'Stevenage is threatened with extinction' and we entirely agree with what you say, and that 'the question of Stevenage is of more far-reaching importance than a local matter.'

If we were the People of Stevenage we would FIGHT THE DICTATORSHIP LABOUR GOVERNMENT with every means at our disposal, and NEVER GIVE UP THE FIGHT AT ANY COST. WRITE to all the MPs and tell them that you will FIGHT to the BITTER END to save Stevenage from spoliation and ruin...

I am sorry I can't give my address, as it is against Army Rules to write about politics.

I am

Yours sincerely

(Signed) Sgt. Frank Truth"

Most national newspapers also took the opportunity to use the satellite town story as a means of attacking the government. This had the effect of adding to the confusion and ambivalence in many minds, as the false assumption grew that all those who opposed the new town plan were Conservatives, while its supporters must be Socialists.

The clash of cultures, exacerbated by the press and the political parties, caused attitudes to polarise, so that there could be no middle way. The cult of "Englishness" still exerted a powerful influence over people of all classes. Its main tenets - glorification of the rural scene, disdain for urban life, nostalgia for the past - may have originated in the public schools, but they were accepted by people from all backgrounds. Even though, by the mid-twentieth century, the majority of English people were living in towns and cities, a vision of village life remained in most minds as the ideal existence. Cutting across nostalgia, the Socialist government placed the harsh facts before the nation. Many thousands of people were homeless. Even before the bombing and destruction of cities, evidence of appalling and degrading living conditions was indisputable. New approaches were needed, which would by-pass both the evolutionary processes of tradition and the market-oriented forces of capitalism. Taking the garden city movement pioneered by Ebenezer Howard as a model, the government proposed utilising modern planning techniques to provide those who moved into the satellite towns with up-to-date homes in a pleasantly landscaped environment.

The unfortunate polarisation of attitudes made it difficult for those who could support some of the arguments on both sides. For many, including Morgan and Elizabeth, the destruction of the countryside - and of so much countryside - was the crucial factor in their opposition to the proposed new town. For other local people, the major objections were: the compulsory purchase and destruction of perfectly good houses, for which compensation at 1939, rather than 1946, prices would be paid; the loss of good agricultural land, at a time when the nation was desperately short of food; and the undemocratic appointment of an Advisory Board, or Development Corporation, with far-reaching powers to oversee the building of the new town, thus by-passing the local council.

Concern was felt too, in the surrounding villages, about the effects of a new town in their midst. For centuries Hitchin had been the market and administrative centre of North Hertfordshire, all roads, literally and metaphorically, leading to it. Now there were anguished debates as to whether the establishment of a protective green belt all round Stevenage would also have the effect of causing rural stagnation in the villages.

THE FORSTER COUNTRY CAMPAIGNS

Eventually, after strenuous representations from the Stevenage Urban District Council, a Public Enquiry opened on October 8th 1946. When he had heard all the depositions the Minister, Lewis Silkin, decided that the new town should go ahead. There was strong feeling, both locally and nationally, that the result was a foregone conclusion and some said that the Enquiry had been a farce. Sponsored by the Hitchin Branch of the National Farmers' Union and by the Stevenage Residents' Association, three local men, William Vernon Franklin (Frank's son), of Rook's Nest Farm, George Hearn of Coreys Mount and Michael Robert Tetley of the Priory (the former Rectory), appealed to the High Court against the decision, on the grounds that Mr Silkin had made up his mind before hearing the objections. On February 20th 1947 Mr Justice Henn Collins upheld their appeal, saying that the question was raised whether Mr Silkin had acted as an honest judge.

The jubilation was short-lived. On July 25th 1947, following an appeal by Mr Silkin to the House of Lords, the judgement in favour of Franklin, Hearn and Tetley was dismissed, and the Stevenage New Town (Designation) order made by the Minister on 11th November 1946 became law. Ironically, one man who had been instrumental in bringing about the Town and Country Planning Act was William Jowitt, appointed Lord Chancellor in 1945 with the title Baron Jowitt of Stevenage.

During the course of the previous two years certain important concessions had been made with regard to the New Town Plan, notably improved compensation for those whose homes would be compulsorily purchased, and some revision to the original plan. The land, to the north of Rooks Nest was, for the moment, reprieved. But the appointment of a Development Corporation went ahead, to the annoyance of the Stevenage Urban District Council, who were not consulted and whose views were ignored. The first Chairman of the Corporation was to be Clough Williams-Ellis, who later achieved fame for building an Italianate village at Portmeirion, North Wales.

142

Soon after their appointment, Williams-Ellis and some other members of the Corporation visited Rooks Nest, where Morgan and Elizabeth hoped that, by showing them the delicate beauty of the countryside, in this "little piece of England" they might persuade them to see matters in a different light. The visit was not a success, the gulf of understanding between the two parties yawning like a crevasse. Elizabeth heard Morgan muttering, "Fourth-rate, fourth-rate," as he observed the distinguished visitors on their unenthusiastic tour, and ever after she delighted in recounting Morgan's instructions to her, "Hide the gin, Elizabeth, we shall need it when they've gone."

The building of the new town then proceeded apace. Some Stevenage residents took their now substantial compensation and moved out. The Tetleys left the Priory, after which it was used, not to house homeless families from London, but as a residence for successive chairmen or officials of the Development Corporation. Over the years other houses were demolished, including Sishes, Highfield, former home of the Postons, "The Mutual Friend" public house and the former Guild of Arts and Literature, both closely associated with Dickens, most of the properties in London Road and the whole of Bedwell Lane. Clarence Elliott's internationally famous Six Hills Nursery was destroyed, in common with many small-holdings and dwellings. It was as if the planners, like the British in Morgan's Chandrapore, were incapable of going round anything, but could only move in straight lines; "...the bungalows are disposed along roads that intersect at right angles."

The destruction of wildlife habitats was immeasurable. It was heart-breaking each spring to watch birds building their nests and bringing food to their fledglings, in the knowledge that bulldozers were poised to rip them out of existence.

As the first arrivals moved in to the newly-built houses, the people of Stevenage welcomed them. To their lasting honour, the churches organised teams of visitors to greet every newcomer and to help build one community. People were also brought together through cultural and leisure

143

THE FORSTER COUNTRY CAMPAIGNS

groups, such as The Lytton Players, founded by Dr Deneys Swayne or The Stevenage Music Society founded by Elizabeth Poston and others. She became its president and supported its activities in a variety of venues in both Old and New Stevenage.

Although the country close to Rooks Nest was spared development for the moment, it did suffer two dramatic changes. In the 1950's a chain of pylons was planted in its fields, as part of the national grid. There was regret about

47. Landscape with pylons.

their visual effect but, after initial horror, Morgan took a philosophical view, christening them "the naked ladies" and always referring to them in this irreverent fashion when he visited Rooks Nest. The other visual disturbance was the appearance of the New Lister Hospital in Coreys Mill Lane. This stark glass and concrete building seems to float like a huge white ship at anchor in the fields, visible for miles. Its arrival was a great blessing to the people of Stevenage, who had formerly to rely on the valiant, but inadequately-housed Lister Hospital at Hitchin. It was through the old Lister Hospital that Elizabeth first met a young distant cousin, Dr Robin Poston, who had known Morgan at Kings College. The friendship which developed between the two Postons was important to both.

From Cambridge to Stevenage is a convenient journey by rail and Morgan was able to visit Rooks Nest frequently. His eminence as a literary and public figure was now immense and when, after travelling to America in 1947, he settled in at Kings College he was, says his biographer P.N. Furbank, "an

144

object of pilgrimage." In spite of this he continued his links with Rooks Nest and the country of his childhood. His fame was a source of amusement to the Franklin family. Mrs Franklin and her daughter Babs used to look out of the window at Rooks Nest Farm when they knew he was coming, to see who was with him. On one occasion, when a young American, aged about thirty, brought him by car, Frank said jovially to Morgan, "The Yanks think more of you than we do, don't they?" Frank was a great reader himself, but found Morgan's books "heavy old stuff." Frank Franklin's death in 1949 was a great personal loss to Morgan, but he kept in touch with the family, through Frank's daughters Babs and Doris, for the rest of his life.

Morgan's Christmas present list for 1947 included the names of Elizabeth Poston and William Jowitt, the Rector's son, now Lord Chancellor of England, who also retained his affection for his childhood home. When the artist Mabel Culley, whose sister had once taught Elizabeth, published a collection of her pictures under the title A *Stevenage Picturebook*, the foreword was contributed by William Jowitt and included the words "For the place which still holds my heart."

In August 1952, during one of his visits to Rooks Nest, Morgan went with Elizabeth to the deserted village of Minsden, near St Paul's Walden, where the ruined chapel was being preserved as a memorial to the respected local Historian, Reginald Hine. Morgan was unimpressed, commenting in his *Commonplace Book*: "Hine - a boring buffer -: 'Hitchin Worthies': Have just visited the odd ruined town.Aug.52" Some years previously Elizabeth had rebuffed Hine when he called at Rooks Nest proposing to write about her in a forthcoming publication. Understandably offended, he withdrew, telling her that she had missed the chance of being recorded for posterity.

At this period Elizabeth was composing and writing prolifically, increasingly in demand as a performer, and as an authority on English music. In 1947 the BBC invited her to become one of the distinguished panel of musicians, writers and broadcasters who were to advise on the creation of its

145

new Third Programme. The excitement and creativity of those days coloured the rest of her life.

Morgan often noted down his thoughts in the *Commonplace Book*, part diary, part note-book, which he had kept intermittently from 1925. In 1958, he fell to musing about his novel *Howards End*;

> "*Howards End*, my best novel and approaching a good novel. Very elaborate and all-pervading plot that is seldom tiresome or forced, range of characters, social sense, wit, wisdom, colour. Have only just discovered why I don't care for it: not a single character in it for whom I care...Perhaps the house in H.E. for which I once did care, took the place of people and now that I no longer care for it their barrenness has become evident."

This is a curious comment, given Morgan's frequent visits to Rooks Nest and the obvious affection in which he held both the house and its inhabitants. In 1956, when his biography of his Aunt Monie, *Marianne Thornton*, was published he had taken a copy to the Postons, autographing it "With love to my Rooksnest dears" and pressing a daisy flower below his signature. Elizabeth later typed the following note, which still covers the fly-leaf: "NB The daisy from the lawn at Rooks Nest with which her [sic] did a favourite childhood's trick is fragile - please kindly keep under cover and from handling. EP"

On January 1st 1959, Morgan was eighty. A luncheon was held in his honour at Kings on January 9th, an enjoyable occasion which was attended by Elizabeth and many distinguished guests, as well as Morgan's cousin Florence Whichelo, who commented on "the marvellous relaxed atmosphere" adding, "Everyone today thought how well and young you looked."

During the year anxiety mounted over the Development Corporation's proposals to make compulsory purchase orders on one hundred and sixty acres of farmland near Rooks Nest in order to build houses. Morgan wrote in his *Commonplace Book*: "...on returning to Cambridge I heard from Elizabeth Poston that Rooks Nest, so long protected by me, is to be destroyed and this has reminded me of the impending destruction of the countryside, the home, and perhaps of the family."

146

In fact the planners had specifically excluded the house from compulsory purchase but, as a reporter in the *Guardian* newspaper wrote on 19th October 1960: "...many objectors feel that the surrounding countryside is inseparable from the immortality of the house." The *Guardian* article, which featured a photograph of Rooks Nest, included the historic statement: "There is special interest in this countryside because part of it is Rooks Nest Farm, [sic] the Forster Country of *Howards End*." Thus the name "Forster Country" had its genesis not in the *Times* as is commonly believed, but in the *Guardian*.

The feared destruction did not take place, but other changes were occurring. The owner of Rooks Nest, Mrs Poyntz-Stewart, died after a lonely and distressing old age, leaving all her property to Niel, who was incapable of taking responsibility for it. The Court of Protection, who looked after his affairs, decided to sell Rooks Nest and Elizabeth took out a mortgage to buy it. She found the financial burden very hard to bear and had serious doubts about the future. In 1961, to her complete surprise, Morgan asked her to allow him to

48. Rooks Nest House
in the 1960's

pay off the mortgage. Her mother, Clementine, wrote to him on December 14th 1961:

> "My dear Morgy,
> I can scarcely see to write to you! being quite blinded by marvellous news that you have so more than generously paid off the mortgage on this most dear house. You cannot possibly imagine the relief it is to me! Quite the most wonderful Christmas gift that life has held for me. I cannot attempt to put all my gratitude into words, or for my dear Elizabeth too and can only add my heartfelt and most grateful love.
> Clementine Poston.

In 1961, Morgan had been seriously ill, but recovered, and was able to return to his rooms at Kings. On December 14, as Clementine was writing to him, he made a note in his *Commonplace Book*; "How peaceful it is here, with the West Hackhurst clock still ticking and the Rooksnest fire irons still warm in the hearth." Frank Franklin's daughters, Babs and Doris, had written wishing him a speedy recovery, and were invited to see him at Kings. They were particularly impressed by the cracked cups in which tea was served.

The relationship between the Postons and Morgan continued to increase in affection. After he visited them early in 1963, Clementine wrote, on March 18th,

> "Very dear Morgy,
> This is only a little post-script to your lovely little time with us and to say what a lovely...time it was. No germ could dare work its evil deeds in the face of such a happy time! and thank you deeply a 1000 times for the quite unnecessary gifts of wine and whisky, E and I are plotting to [...] the first and then be fighting fit. Bless you very dear Morgy for such a very kind thought
> I do hope your travels will be the very happiest success. Let me know when you are again in residence!
> (No answer of course)
> So very much love
> Clementine Poston

On Morgan's ninetieth birthday, on January 1st 1969, he was awarded the Order of Merit in the New Year's honours list. Later that month there was a celebration luncheon, organised by King's College, at which he was presented with a leather-bound copy of *Aspects of E.M.Forster*, edited by Oliver Stallybrass. Again, Elizabeth was one of the guests, who were fewer in number than on his eightieth birthday, in view of his now frail health.

It was clear to his friends that Morgan could not live very much longer. Elizabeth, ever conscious of his importance to the nation as well as to his former Hertfordshire home, often talked to him about a suitable memorial. He was at first evasive, saying, "My dear Elizabeth, I cannot conceive of this world without me in it." To which she replied, "Neither can I, but it would be so much easier for me if I knew about this."

Eventually he agreed to discuss the subject and together they planned a sundial plaque on the front wall of Rooks Nest, beneath Morgan's former nursery window, with the inscription: "E.M.Forster, Clementine Poston, Elizabeth Poston, lived here and loved this place."

On 7th June 1970, Elizabeth was sitting in Morgan's chair in the drawing room at Rooks Nest, looking out at the garden, watching the hollyhocks blooming against the window. She was thinking of how Morgan always maintained that hollyhocks have faces, when the radio announcer said, "We regret to announce the death of Mr E.M.Forster at 4 am this morning, very peacefully..." Although there was no wind the hollyhocks turned their faces towards her.

49. Dovecote made from the felled wych elm

10
THE FIGHT CONTINUES

Morgan's death left a vacuum at Rooks Nest. For Elizabeth, a major loss was their shared laughter; they both had a robust sense of humour. She also missed him as a vigorous ally in the continuing battle against the forces of modern bureaucracy. But there were immediate practical matters to be attended to, which gave her little time for regret. In any case, self-pity was not one of her characteristics. She was only too well aware that her mother's rapidly declining health and loss of independence meant that she herself would be increasingly confined to her home. Times had changed; it was no longer possible to acquire servants to help run the house, even if there had been the money to pay them. With typical optimism, Elizabeth accepted what life was offering, turning her attention to the house which Morgan had loved so much and which was now becoming her own chief focus.

The house was always in need of attention. Routine maintenance was carried out by the faithful Jock Briars, who would also turn his hand to more unusual tasks if required. He and his future son-in-law, Albert Haggar, although no plumbers, installed the enormous downstairs bath in the former dairy opposite the kitchen. Elizabeth, always keen to have modern conveniences, was determined to do nothing which would alter the essential character of the house. She had long disliked the layers of paint, legacy of the Victorian age, which covered doors, stair-rails and wood panelling, and herself undertook the task of gently scraping away the offending surface, to reveal the golden wood beneath.

The countryside was a constant delight; Elizabeth took pleasure in driving out to visit her many friends in the Forster Country villages or, even more enjoyable, to set off with her cairns, Pinky and Comfort, to walk across the fields to Chesfield. When Pinky died, she buried the little body under a bramble bush at the foot of the donkeys' field, then

150

assuaged her grief by composing *Blackberry Fold: Requiem for a Dog* as a memorial. Comfort, Pinky's daughter, had been bred at Rooks Nest, acquiring her unusual name at birth. One dog puppy after another emerged into the world, until at last a bitch appeared, prompting the comment, "Well, that's a comfort, anyway."

Although circumstances now prevented her from leaving home for long, Elizabeth was very much in touch with the wider world of the arts. Her music was accorded increasing respect from fellow musicians. *The Second Penguin Book of Christmas Carols*, published in 1970 and *The Faber Book of French Folksongs*, published in 1972, were the results of painstaking scholarship and almost soul-destroying difficulties. With very little assistance, she had to attend to her incontinent and confused mother during the day, waiting until darkness brought merciful sleep to Clementine before she could return to her music. Slowly, night after night, the work was completed.

This was a time of enormous stress, but Elizabeth refused to allow herself to be overcome by physical weariness, or by the sorrowful knowledge that there could be only one outcome for her mother. Family and friends kept in touch by letter, talked to her on the telephone, or came in person to Rooks Nest where laughter and music still reigned, in spite of everything. The learned support of Peter Wright, her editor at Penguin, helped her immeasurably at this time, as did the friendship of Philip and Anthea Craggs, to whom *The Faber Book of French Folksongs* is dedicated. Above all, there was her brother Ralph, to whom she was bound by the strongest ties of affection, although his career as a diplomat often took him out of the country.

Usually, with the devoted help of Mrs Briars, and of old "Auntie" Ethel, who herself was beginning to suffer delusions, Elizabeth managed to cope with the domestic demands which pressed upon her. But when things were really bad, she turned in desperation to Dr Margaret Swayne, the family doctor to whom almost everyone in Stevenage went when in trouble, and that saintly woman did not fail

THE FIGHT CONTINUES

her. Recalling this harrowing time years later, Elizabeth said
simply, "I asked her and she came."

Clementine died in 1971 and was buried in St. Nicholas'
churchyard. She had previously expressed the wish that her
body be carried to the funeral on a farm wagon, but as this
proved impossible to arrange, a more conventional funeral
had to take place. For Elizabeth, to whom all ritual to do with
death was abhorrent, the whole affair was a nightmare, but
she was comforted by the perceptive and sensitive address
given by the Vicar, the Reverend Christopher Weston.

Not long after Clementine's death the strain of the last few
years told on Elizabeth and, as she sat at her writing desk, she
felt a violent stabbing pain in her back: "I thought the IRA
had burst in." She managed to dial 999, then knew no more
until she woke up at the New Lister Hospital. Mrs Briars and
her daughter Anne arrived in time to hear a doctor say, "If
we can't find anything else we'll take out the appendix," at
which a familiar voice, weak but determined, replied, "Oh
no you won't." When it was discovered that she had an
aneurysm, that is a burst ulcer on a main artery, Elizabeth's
chances of survival were considered almost nil. By what can
only be described as a miracle, such was the skill of the
hospital surgeons that she lived, avoiding death by a hair's
breadth.

Lying weakly in a hospital bed, unable to move, Elizabeth
at first found the steady flow of anxious visitors
overwhelming. Then, as her strength returned, so did the
familiar grin and the delight in entertaining an audience, as
she described with relish how, "I almost drowned in my own
blood." When she was well enough, it was arranged that she
should go for convalescence to a convent at Westcliffe near
Clacton. Anne Briars, who drove her there, remembers with
amused affection that Elizabeth, too weak to stand properly,
insisted on stopping the car halfway through the journey so
that she could get out to breathe country air. Grateful though
she was to the Lister Hospital, where she had many friends,
she had longed to escape from her enforced incarceration
indoors. Without open air and the life of the countryside
around her, she felt suffocated.

152

In 1975 Elizabeth was seventy. A birthday party was called for which would also celebrate her recovery from illness and the beginning of a new era in her life. At Joan Littlejohn's suggestion, her good friends, Oliver and Gunnvor Stallybrass arranged a gathering at their London house. Oliver, a distinguished literary scholar, had known Elizabeth since he took up his appointment as editor of the Abinger edition of the works of E.M. Forster. Working from manuscripts in the Forster archive at Kings College, Cambridge and from other sources, he was producing definitive, annotated editions of all Morgan's texts for his publisher, Edward Arnold. The Abinger edition of *Howard's End* had appeared in 1973, with its companion volume, *The Manuscripts of Howard's End*, both invaluable to scholars. Naturally, it had been essential for Oliver to visit the original of Howard's End, since when Elizabeth's help and continuing interest in his work had resulted in warm friendship. For Gunnvor, their first meeting was unforgettable. As she and Oliver approached

50. Elizabeth Poston in her music room at Rooks Nest.

153

the front door of Rooks Nest, a tall, graceful woman, wearing a long dress and holding a posy of wildflowers in her hand came towards them across the grass. For one startled moment, Gunnvor thought that this was Mrs Wilcox, as the words from *Howard's End* leapt into her mind: "She approached just as Helen's letter had described her, trailing noiselessly over the lawn, and there was actually a wisp of hay in her hands."

The birthday party was a happy occasion, with musicians, family, BBC colleagues and local friends coming together to pay tribute to Elizabeth. As always in congenial company, she sparkled, regaling her listeners with hilarious anecdotes from her remarkable career. A highlight of the evening was soprano Caroline Clack's rendering of songs by Peter Warlock and Elizabeth herself. The recital ended with *Cuddle In*, a Yorkshire folksong, and at this point Comfort decided to steal the show by emerging from her basket to snuggle round her mistress' feet.

By coincidence, the party helped her to complete an unfinished project which had been on her mind since the deaths of Morgan and Clementine. The memorial sundial which they had planned together had never been made. Three of them had agreed the words, but to Elizabeth alone fell the melancholy task of completing the dates and commissioning the work. So far, she had been unable to progress any further. After the party, she met the artist Audrey Hammond, who later introduced her to Bob Duvivier. He it was who subsequently designed the plaque and arranged for the lettering to be engraved. The sundial, affixed to the front wall of Rooks Nest, immediately under Morgan's nursery window, has since been photographed by visitors from all over the world.

Elizabeth reached her seventieth birthday, on October 24th 1975. That same month she was saddened by the death of Sir Arthur Bliss, with whom she had worked at the BBC. Since 1953 he had held the office of Master of the Queen's Music; now his place was taken by the youngest man ever to be appointed to this position, the forty-five year old Australian composer Malcolm Williamson. He had been a great

154

admirer of Elizabeth's work since he first heard *Sweet Suffolk Owl* as a boy on the other side of the world. In his judgement she was a greater composer than either Peter Warlock or her mentor, Vaughan Williams.

Hardly had she triumphed over debilitating illness when Elizabeth was faced with another battle. The 1976 Stevenage Master Plan incorporated proposals for the expansion of Stevenage from a target population of 60,000 to one of 80,000. Feelings ran high, since the proposed expansion was seen by many as a distortion of the original plan and, it must be said, as an excuse for the continued existence of the Development Corporation. Those in favour of expansion claimed that it would provide housing for the children of existing residents, as well as boosting the local economy. Elizabeth was one of those who could see that, if these arguments were accepted, there was no logical reason why the expansion of the new town should ever stop, as she explained later in her preface to *The Book of Stevenage;* "He [Forster] knew that 'the red rust creeping' from the brick city - what I know in my time as the galloping cancer of concrete - must be contained within the countryside that provides the city with the food, not only of man's body, but his soul."

51. Elizabeth Poston with Comfort

The 1976 Master Plan envisaged building on the Forster Country and adjacent farmland. There were many local objections, but it was realised that on their own, these might not be sufficiently convincing of the value that the international community placed upon the childhood home of a writer who was revered the world over. Oliver Stallybrass worked with Elizabeth to co-ordinate the response from scholars who were now rallying to the defence of Forster's "little piece of England." On 29th April 1976, a letter from King's College, Cambridge, signed by Oliver Stallybrass and twenty-nine other distinguished persons from four continents, was published in the *Times* newspaper. It began:

155

THE FIGHT CONTINUES

"Our particular concern is the threat to an exceptionally beautiful pocket of countryside which is also part of Britain's cultural heritage. For it adjoins Rooks Nest House, the childhood home of E.M. Forster and the model for *Howard's End*, and was referred to by yourself, Sir, as "The Forster Country" on the occasion some years ago, of a successful campaign for its conservation which Forster himself helped to wage."

It is amusing now to realise that a slip of the pen ascribing coinage of "Forster Country" to the *Times* has gone uncorrected for 15 years, during which the *Guardian* has remained magnanimously silent.

The objections were effective and the Master Plan map was amended to include for the first time the name "Forster Country" on land contiguous with Rooks Nest. To be true to its name, it should have encompassed all the countryside bounded by Rectory Lane, Rooks Nest, Weston, Graveley and the North Road. Part of the problem here lay in the fact that The Forster Country was bisected by the local authority boundary line running between Stevenage and North Herts District. An added complication for the future would arise because only part of the Forster Country was within the Green Belt. However, for the time being it was safe, although building activity on the south side of the Weston Road was proceeding apace; the high hedges now seemed scant protection against the roar of bulldozers ripping through Highfield, Pin Green and Mill Field.

She now lived virtually alone but Elizabeth's life was full. Friends, colleagues, even complete strangers, came constantly to Rooks Nest, to see the original of *Howard's End*, to enjoy the pleasure of Elizabeth's company or to retreat for a while from sorrow. "This good house," one recently-bereaved friend described it, after a comforting afternoon in Elizabeth's music room, watching the wood fire burning in the grate, being plied with tea on a delicate little tray and talking or not, as she felt inclined. Elizabeth always made time for people, even when she was at her busiest, with deadlines looming. She would work all night, rather than turn away a friend, or a timid newcomer who had called on the off-chance of being allowed to see the place which Morgan had immortalised. She brushed aside the

156

possible dangers of inviting strangers into her home, trusting absolutely her own judgement as to who could safely be made welcome and who should be sent away with icy politeness.

In spite of her greatness, Elizabeth was in many ways extremely reticent, even shy. Locally she was known and loved by many who were but dimly aware of her achievements. Inviting her to give a public lecture was usually futile, but Gim Weston did once persuade her to face The Anglican Women's Guild, a small, unintimidating group which met fortnightly in Springfield House, formerly the home of Morgan's erstwhile headmaster at the Grange School, but now used as a community centre. Elizabeth agreed reluctantly, on condition that she need not "give a talk" but would play a tape instead. As she explained to a fascinated audience, "I am all right behind a microphone, but I am terrified of facing you all." The recording which she brought with her was on unofficial loan from the BBC; she had made it at their request for use, she claimed, as autobiographical material after her death. In it she described her life with music, from her earliest memories of her mother's heartbeat and homely sounds such as the ticking of clocks and the birdsong of her native Hertfordshire to her travels across the globe on the track of folk song, ending with a brief glance at her war years with the BBC. Her listeners were enthralled, not least by the knowledge that they were the recipients of a rare privilege.

Christmas was always a particularly strenuous time for Elizabeth. Both her carols, and she herself, were in demand for concerts locally and nationally. *Jesus Christ the Apple Tree*, which she wrote in her teens, had captured many hearts and was becoming one of the most frequently performed carols. She was always delighted when young people appreciated her music. One association which gave her particular pleasure concerned the Ward Freman School at Buntingford, of which she was to write later;

"...a remarkable place I have long been interested in - they have adopted me and I them - charming, enterprising folk artistically go-ahead...Their two patrons have been me and Henry Moore and

THE FIGHT
CONTINUES

they are very sad at his loss. He was very kind to them and let them have marvellous exhibitions of his work from his home at Little Hadham. A year or two ago they built on the Poston Room, (complete with photograph!) for their music wing, and it has always been a very happy relationship. I don't like a Christmas to go by without a visit..."

She tried to remember all her friends at Christmas, especially old or frail local people whose friendship went back to the time when Stevenage was "the village." Little pots of Rooks Nest honey or jam would be wrapped carefully in a piece of last year's Christmas paper and decorated with a sprig of winter jasmine, an ivy leaf or a stem of balsam, to which was added an affectionate message in her distinctive handwriting on the tiniest possible tag. How many of these reminders of Elizabeth are still preserved in the Forster Country or beyond? Many friends collected their presents when they came to Rooks Nest with their own gifts for her, but by Christmas Eve there were always a few packages remaining. Elizabeth, with Comfort beside her, would drive out into the night, to old Alfie's cottage on the way to Weston; then on to Chesfield, where her headlights might illuminate the white plumage of a hunting barn-owl. A little parcel would be left at artist May Bloom's caravan at Crow End; yet another at the council flat in Stevenage where lived old Mrs Adams who once worked for her mother; then on again, until the round was completed, and the loving message of Christmas handed on for another year.

Usually Elizabeth attended Christmas services at the little church at Weston, which she loved for its ancient rural tranquillity. Christmas Day was spent with friends, such as the Pryors, but increasingly, as the years went by, she liked to be home at Rooks Nest by dark, when telephone messages from family and colleagues flowed in. Indeed, it was an unusual day when the telephone did not ring at Rooks Nest. Characteristically, Elizabeth would answer with a distant "Hallo?" uttered as if she were about to expire, but as soon as the caller's voice was recognised, there were exclamations of delight, after which a long, affectionate conversation would ensue, during which she touched amusingly on a range of current events, never hesitating to express her opinion

158

forcibly. She always claimed to dislike the telephone, preferring to write even if it meant delivering the note herself.

Of the great number of people who asked to see her at Rooks Nest, many were Forster scholars or students. She made it a point of honour never to refuse anyone who was genuinely interested, although sometimes this was at considerable inconvenience to her own life. Only when her mother was in the final stages of illness did she find it impossible to allow visitors. Unfortunately this period coincided with the making of the television version of *Howards End* in 1970; under normal circumstances Rooks Nest itself would have been the location, but, disappointingly, a substitute had to be found, not far away, at Ashwell. When she was invited to write the music for the film Elizabeth at first declined but:

> "I relented because I suppose the whole thing was too strong, and because no one else knows the real story. A lifetime - several lifetimes - went into the music: not only the poignancy of the present, but an almost unbearable nostalgia for a past which the book enshrines...Love of place, to the countryman, is curiously strong and this old house has been much loved."

The score, which she wrote in such difficult circumstances, is considered by fellow musicians to be among her finest work.

Many eminent literary scholars made their way to the house. Oliver and Gunnvor Stallybrass were perhaps the leading "Forsterians" as Elizabeth dubbed them, but others included Professor George Thomson from Ottawa University, author of *The Fiction of E.M.Forster* and Professor Wilfred Stone from Stanford, USA, who wrote the widely acclaimed study *The Cave and the Mountain*. Autographed copies of their work, together with their continuing support for the campaigns to protect the Forster Country, bore witness to the esteem in which they held the house and its chatelaine. Tragically, Oliver Stallybrass died at the peak of his career, in 1979. His friendship had meant much to Elizabeth; his kind, scholarly presence at Cambridge a continuing link with Morgan. It was with great sorrow that

159

she went, on April 28th, to take part in his memorial service at King's College Chapel.

1979 was notable also as the one hundredth anniversary of Morgan's birth. Stevenage Museum, whose curator at that time was Colin Dawes, with Rosemary Gilmour as his assistant, were planning an exhibition, for which I undertook to make a tape-slide programme. Elizabeth agreed to read the commentary, but in one of her fits of shyness, insisted that all the advance publicity should state "commentary by a friend of Forster," to stave off an invasion by the local press. I spent a happy time researching in the library of King's and at Hatfield House, talking to local contacts and photographing scenes and buildings which Morgan had known as a child. Elizabeth was very enthusiastic about the project. She chose George Butterworth's *On Wenlock Edge* for the background music, as being suitably English, and in the knowledge that Morgan had admired Housman's *A Shropshire Lad*. One Sunday afternoon we met in the drawing room at Rooks Nest to record the commentary; as the record of *On Wenlock Edge* was played, Elizabeth looked severely at the revolving disc and remarked, "That horn is a little flat," adding, in response to my look of surprise, "It would be perfectly acceptable to most people, but I have an unusually acute ear."

Despite a series of eleventh-hour crises, the official opening of the Forster Centenary Exhibition was a great success. Guests included Dr Michael Halls and Dr Elizabeth Heine from King's College, Cambridge and Frank Franklin's daughters, Babs Franklin and Doris Guest. For some reason the air-conditioning system was out of order, with the result that, on a warm July night, perspiration stood out on all faces, not least on Elizabeth's, as she watched the tape-slide programme for the third time. After that, her enthusiasm knew no bounds and she brought Forsterians from all over the country to the museum throughout the exhibition period. The inevitable publicity resulted in a record number of visitors to Rooks Nest; at the end of the year she estimated that approaching 2,000 people had come to the house and on to the Forster Country beyond. The extra work in which this

160

involved her was considerable, but she relished it as a way of promoting "the cause," the preservation of the Forster country.

For many years, Elizabeth had been intent on leaving Rooks Nest to the nation so that it could continue as an inspiration to future generations. She also saw this as a way of protecting the house in its countryside. As she grew older, she became almost obsessed with Rooks Nest, speaking of its unique healing quality: "It is a wonderful house. People have come for all sorts of reasons...We can't *all* imagine it, there is some kind of goodness or strength here." Her original plan, to leave the house to the National Trust, was under review, since it was now clear that a considerable endowment would also be necessary for upkeep of the property. With this knowledge, Elizabeth decided to keep her options open, while investigating other possible ways of safeguarding it for posterity.

As Elizabeth pondered on the future of the house, she became curious about its past. She wanted to learn more about the Howards who had disappeared so mysteriously in 1882, after 300 years. So we began to search at the Hertfordshire County Record Office and were delighted to find so many records relating to Rooks Nest, including a beautifully hand-coloured Chesfield estate map with "Mr Howard's" clearly marked. Elizabeth revelled in the thrill of the chase as we pounced on any scrap of information which brought us closer to the Howards. After a visit to the Public Record Office, where we tracked down two more wills, we were able to draw up a family tree. We now had a fair amount of factual information, but of course nothing to indicate what the Howards were like as people. "We shall

52. Rhubarb pots in the kitchen garden at Rooks Nest.

never know what they looked like," Elizabeth would say wistfully, and we would conjure up images of fair-haired Saxon farmers, strong, silent men who nurtured their land and were, as Morgan wrote in *Howards End*, "England's hope." There were reasons for believing that the last Howard might have emigrated to Australia or New Zealand during the farming decline of the 1880's and we occasionally fantasised on tracing their descendants, who would complete the story by returning to "Mr Howard's." So far this dream remains unrealised.

Another link with the past had been broken with the death of Comfort, the courageous little cairn. Elizabeth was grief-stricken, not only at the loss of a beloved companion, but also because Comfort was the last living connection with her mother, with Morgan and the friends of a past era. She wrote:

> "Sixteen years is quite a slice of life and she was close through all it contained. There was never a shadow on our perfect happiness together. She died in my arms, loving, serene and trustful as she had lived. I dug her little grave and laid her in it, anonymous now, but daffodils in the spring."

Those who have dogs of their own will understand Elizabeth's resolve never to have another, even though this would mean that she would be completely alone in the house. However, a russet-coloured miracle by the name of Polly saved her from complete desolation. Polly was rescued from certain death on the Euston Road by a BBC friend, who brought her to Rooks Nest where she stayed as trusty companion for the rest of Elizabeth's life.

Now in her late seventies, Elizabeth was working harder than ever. She evolved a system by which she rose at 5 am, opened the back door of the lobby for the postman, then hoovered and dusted, completing her household chores well before the arrival of any visitors. Much in demand for reviewing, she still continued with her own compositions and made radio and television appearances.

The garden remained an unfailing pleasure. She was at her most relaxed and happy when working outdoors with David Ginn, the trusted friend, who tended the Rooks Nest garden. The miles of hedge were for some years looked after by George Davey, a lonely countryman stranded in the new town, to whom Elizabeth gave practical help and staunch support in the face of officialdom. Much of the weeding she did herself, often working in the dusk of a summer evening when all was still and she could savour the scent of roses while listening to the late song of a thrush and the subdued twitterings of little hedgerow birds as they settled down for the night. From the field would come the harsh call of a pheasant, and, lifting her head, she would say gently, "Is that you, Chuffy?" for one particularly beautiful cock pheasant was very tame, often arriving at the back door to be hand fed by Elizabeth, who took great pains to hide him from the shooting fraternity.

When it became too dark to see, Elizabeth would walk down to say goodnight to her donkeys, Fairy and Nonnie, stroking their rough faces as she watched the moon light up the Forster Country stretching out below. On one such evening, as she went back towards the house, some slight movement made her shine her torch into the air ahead, to find herself face to face with a tawny owl. For a split second they stared at one another and, Elizabeth said, "I saw into the eye and brain of an owl."

53. Elizabeth Poston and her donkeys, Fairy and Nonnie.

THE FIGHT CONTINUES

For first-time visitors, Rooks Nest on a winter's evening was an unforgettable experience. Unaware of behind-the-scenes battles to keep the Aga stoked up, and coal and logs fetched from the shed across a yard made treacherous by layers of ice, they had eyes for nothing but the fire-light playing on ancient walls, the learned clutter of books and music and most of all, the joyful smile on Elizabeth's face, reflecting her pleasure in meeting new people. An entry from my diary for 3rd April 1983 is a typical example of the Rooks Nest effect:

> "While tea was in preparation two young people (Forsterians) came on bicycles. One, Edward, thin, fairly tall...Girl's name I didn't catch...He very anxious to know about us...obviously believes we are all part of an enchanted circle - said, 'And you are all friends here,' to which I replied facetiously, 'We are all eccentric,' to bring him down to earth a little, but secretly I feel the same - it is all rather magical. We had to rush off before conversation could develop. As we turned out of Weston Road by St.Nicholas' Church, saw Japanese man, woman and child heading for Rooks Nest on foot."

Subsequently the young man, Edward, sent Elizabeth a small acrylic of a view from a window, which she kept always on the kitchen table. The Japanese visitors wrote some months later to say that they had named their new baby Meg after Margaret Schlegel in *Howard's End*.

As a result of the Japanese connection, Elizabeth became interested in their music, and was delighted to receive, via King's College, tapes of some Japanese children's songs. I received an SOS to bring a cassette player and one summer evening we sat with windows wide open, in the darkening kitchen of Rooks Nest, while a chorus of Japanese voices poured forth into the Hertfordshire night. An occasional little pale moth fluttered by and Polly snored gently as, behind us, the dark house, which had heard so much in its three hundred years, received into itself these new oriental sounds.

The vigour and clarity of her mind, her sense of fun and her joy in life made Elizabeth seem ageless, but 1985 heralded her eightieth birthday. Plans were made for a major celebration, to be held at Berkhamsted, where she had many

164

associates as well as being vice-president of the Berkhamsted Music Society. The occasion was to be an important one musically, in that her song cycle *Autobiography* was to be given its first public performance, with Brian Rayner Cook and Christopher Robinson. The audience which gathered on October 12th 1985 brought together people from all facets of Elizabeth's life: members of her family, BBC colleagues, eminent musicians, literary scholars and friends from the Forster Country villages. No one was in any doubt that the music would be superb, but the reality surpassed expectation. In the intervals between songs Elizabeth, in sparkling form, reminisced about her life, including as she always did, a reference to the Forster Country. It was a unique occasion, not least because of the pride and affection which beamed from the faces of her audience.

A year later, Elizabeth's eighty-first birthday was spent in the Lister Hospital, where she stayed three weary months recovering from a fall which left her with multiple injuries. Even worse, underlying her physical pain, was the anguish she was suffering after the recent death of her brother, Ralph, a sorrow from which she never recovered. But the loving support of very many friends, coupled with her determination to return to Rooks Nest, helped her to win through to a brief convalescence with the Revd. and Mrs Robert Poston, Robin's parents, after which she went home to make a gradual, almost complete recovery.

During the long months of illness, friends had helped in various ways. One whose practical support had been invaluable was fireman Tom Allan, who continued devotedly to watch over Elizabeth even after her health was better. On the morning of March 17th 1987 he called as usual at Rooks Nest, to find her in the chair by the fire in her music room, deeply unconscious. After giving her the kiss of life, he took her to the hospital, where a massive stroke was diagnosed. She did not regain consciousness, but had, to all intents and purposes, died as she had always wished, at home at Rooks Nest, while working on her current commission, a carol book to be published by the Sheldrake Press. Those of us who were with her at the end, watching as

165

THE FIGHT CONTINUES

she lay tranquilly on her side, will never forget the desolate unreality of those few hours; but at least we were given the opportunity of seeing her again, to say, each in our own way, our last goodbyes.

There was no funeral. Her body was willed to medical science. Instead, a memorial service was held at St. Nicholas' Church, whither she had skipped as a child in her little button boots to hear ruddy-cheeked Rector Jowitt preach. But, as she herself had planned, this sorrowful occasion was transformed by music into one of joyful thanksgiving. Members of the Stevenage Music Society, augmented by other singers, formed the choir. Brian Rayner Cook sang again *Sweet Suffolk Owl* and *The Bellman's Song* which, only eighteen months ago, had been so happily received at the eightieth birthday celebrations. The address was given by Dr Malcolm Williamson, Master of the Queen's Music, who concluded with the words, "May her dear soul rest in peace, united with the radix of the Apple Tree." As the whole congregation joined in the singing of *Jesus Christ the Apple Tree*, we realised with fresh understanding the poignancy of the final verse:

"This fruit doth make my soul to thrive,
It keeps my dying faith alive;
Which makes my soul in haste to be
With Jesus Christ the apple tree."

54. Irises at Rooks Nest

11
SUCCESSION

A wet evening in Royston on 18th May 1985 had been the unlikely setting for a seminal meeting between Elizabeth Poston and Malcolm Williamson. Long an admirer of her work, he was at once captivated by her personality, becoming a frequent visitor to Rooks Nest as their friendship deepened. When she died, leaving the Sheldrake Press carol book half-completed, it was decided to invite another composer, whose music complemented her own, to finish the work; the obvious choice was Malcolm Williamson. The book was published in the autumn of 1988, a token of the delights to come as the hidden treasure of Elizabeth's music is revealed to the world.

After all the agonising over its future Rooks Nest remained in the Poston family, to the general approbation of the neighbourhood. In a district which had seen so much change, continuity was important. Then, by a quirk of fate worthy of a Forster novel, it became necessary to let the house and Malcolm Williamson found himself living there, drawing inspiration from it as Morgan and Elizabeth had before him.

As for the Forster Country, sinister little notices were again appearing on fence posts, signalling the intention of private companies to build on the land. Some erosion of the surrounding fields had already taken place, but now developers were preparing to move into the heart of the Forster Country. Events followed a familiar pattern: a storm of objections to the proposals; refusal of the initial planning application, followed by an appeal to the Department of the Environment by the developers. The appeal hearing began on September 21st 1988. As the participants assembled in the Stevenage Council Chamber all the lights went out, seeming to some of those present to symbolise the spiritual darkness which would engulf us if the Forster Country were lost.

SUCCESSION

55. Gunnvor Stallybrass looking towards the Forster Country from Rooks Nest, at the inauguration of the Friends of the Forster Country, May 21st 1989

56. Malcolm Williamson (second from left) with the Mayor of Stevenage, Mrs Hilda Lawrence and Sir Norman Lindop (right) at the unveiling of a Hertfordshire County Council plaque at the entrance to Rooks Nest House, 21st December 1989.

In April 1989 the long-awaited judgement was delivered: the Department of the Environment inspector recommended upholding the Stevenage Borough Council's decision not to allow development in the Forster Country. Jubilation among the objectors was tempered by the knowledge that this was but a temporary reprieve; other planning applications were in the pipeline. Thus, The Friends of the Forster Country came into being, with the aim "To preserve for all time the open green space to the north of Stevenage, part of which is known as the Forster Country."

The final battle is not yet fought. The story of the Forster Country is unfinished. Will it succumb, as Elizabeth Poston feared, to "the cancer of concrete," or will it live as countryside which we, with E.M. Forster, "still think the loveliest in England"?

BIBLIOGRAPHY
OF WORKS MENTIONED IN THE TEXT

ARMA, Paul
Faber book of French folksongs -
arranged and translated by
Elizabeth Poston.
Faber, 1972

ARNIM, Elizabeth von
Elizabeth and her German garden.
Macmillan, 1898

ASHBY, Margaret
The Book of Stevenage
Barracuda, 1982

CULLEY, Mabel
A Stevenage picture book

FORSTER, E.M.
Commonplace book, edited by
Philip Gardner
Scolar Press, 1985

FORSTER, E.M.
A Diary for Timothy (filmscript)
Crown Film Unit, 1945

FORSTER, E.M.
Howards End
Edward Arnold, 1910

FORSTER, E.M.
The Manuscripts of Howards End,
edited by Oliver Stallybrass.
Edward Arnold, 1973

FORSTER, E.M.
Marianne Thornton; a domestic
biography, 1797 - 1887.
Edward Arnold, 1956

FORSTER, E.M.
The Longest Journey
Edward Arnold, 1907

FORSTER, E.M.
A Passage to India
Edward Arnold, 1924

FORSTER, E.M.
A Room with a view
Edward Arnold, 1908

FORSTER, E.M.
Two cheers for democracy
Edward Arnold, 1951

FORSTER, E.M.
Where angels fear to tread
Edward Arnold, 1905

FURBANK, P.N.
E.M. Forster, a life
Secker & Warburg, 1977-8 (two
volumes)

LOMAX, Alan
The Penguin Book of American
folksongs - Piano arrangements by
Elizabeth Poston
Penguin, 1964

POSTON, Elizabeth
The Baby's song book
Bodley Head, 1972

POSTON, Elizabeth
The Penguin book of Christmas
carols
Penguin, 1965

POSTON, Elizabeth
The Second Penguin book of
Christmas carols
Penguin, 1970

POSTON, Elizabeth and
WILLIAMSON, Malcolm
Christmas Carols
Simon and Schuster, 1988

STALLYBRASS, Oliver, editor
Aspects of E.M. Forster
Edward Arnold, 1969

STONE, Wilfred
The Cave and the mountain
Oxford University Press, 1966

THOMSON, George H.
The Fiction of E. M. Forster
Wayne State University Press,
Detroit, 1967

INDEX

Page numbers in *italics* indicate illustrations.

174